P9-CBS-059

A HISTORICAL READER

The
Civil War

nextext

Table of Contents

Throughout the reader, vocabulary words appear in boldface
type and are footnoted. Specialized or technical words and phrases
appear in lightface type and are footnoted.

Slavery Divides
the Nation

An English Woman's Account of Plantation Life

BY HARRIET MARTINEAU

The divisions in the United States that led to the Civil War had their beginnings very early in the nation's history. The colonies that formed the Southern states developed differently from those in the North. The economy of the South depended upon its agricultural products, cotton and tobacco. Manufacturing developed in the North. Even at the time of the writing of the Constitution, nearly a hundred years before the war, the Southern states feared the greater power of the North. While several of the Constitution's writers wanted to end the institution of slavery, they could not form a union without it. By the 1830s, when the English author Harriet Martineau visited America, slavery was essential to the Southern way of life.

There was no end to the kind cautions given me against traveling through the Southern States, not only on account of my opinions on slavery, but because of the badness of the roads and the poverty of the wayside accommodations. There was so much of this that my companion and I held a consultation one day, in our room at Washington, spreading out the map, and surveying the vast extent of country we proposed to traverse before meeting my relatives at New-Orleans. We found that neither was afraid, and afterward that there was no cause for fear, except to persons who are annoyed by irregularity and the absence of comfort. The evil **prognostications**[1] went on multiplying as we advanced; but we learned to consider them as mere voices on the mountain of our enterprise, which must not deter us from accomplishing it. We had friends to visit at Charleston and Columbia, South Carolina; Augusta, Georgia; Montgomery, Alabama; and Mobile. At Richmond we were cautioned about the journey into South Carolina; at Charleston we were met with dreadful reports of traveling in Georgia; in Georgia people spoke of the horrors of Alabama, and so on; and, after all, nothing could well be easier than the whole undertaking. I do not remember a single difficulty that occurred all the way. There was much fatigue, of course. In going down from Richmond to Charleston with a party of friends, we were nine days on the road, and had only three nights' rest. Throughout the journey we were obliged to accommodate ourselves to the stage hours,[2] setting off sometimes in the evening, sometimes at midnight; or, of all uncomfortable seasons, at two or three in the morning. . . . In Alabama, some of the passengers in the stage were Southern gentlemen coming from New-York, in comparison with whose fatigues ours were nothing. I think they had then traveled eleven days and nights with very short intervals of rest, and the

---

[1] **prognostications**—forecasts; predictions.

[2] stage hours—the stagecoach schedule.

badness of the roads at the end of a severe winter had obliged them to walk a good deal. They looked dreadfully haggard and nervous, and we heard afterward that one of them had become incessantly convulsed in the face after we had left them. It is not necessary, of course, to proceed without stopping in such a way as this; but it is necessary to be patient of fatigue to travel in the South at all.

Yet I was very fond of these long journeys. The traveler (if he be not an **abolitionist**[3]) is perfectly secure of good treatment, and fatigue and indifferent fare are the only evils which need be anticipated. . . .

The American can conceive of nothing more dismal than a pine-barren on a rainy day; but the profound tranquillity made it beautiful to me, whose rainy days have been almost all spent in cities, amid the rumbling of hackney-coaches, the clink of pattens,[4] the gurgle of spouts, and the flitting by of umbrellas. It is very different in the pine-barrens. The sandy soil absorbs the rain, so that there is no mud; the pines stand meekly drooping, as if waiting to be fed; the drip is noiseless; and the brooks and pools are seen bubbling clear, or quietly filling, while not a wing cleaves the air, each bird nestling in the covert of its domestic tree. When the rain ceases towards evening, the whole region undergoes a change. If a parting ray from the west pierces the woods, the stems look lilac in the moist light; the vines glitter before they shake off their last drops; the redbird startles the eye; the butterflies come abroad in clouds; the frogs grow noisy, and all nature wakens up fresh as from her siesta. The planter may be seen on his pacing white horse in

---

[3] **abolitionist**—one who favors getting rid of slavery.
[4] pattens—shoes with a high sole for walking in mud.

a glade of the wood, or **superintending**[5] the negroes who are repairing the fence of his estate. One black holds the large dibble, with which the holes for the stakes are made; others are warming their hands at the fire which blazes on the ground; many hands to do slovenly work. While any light is left, the driver is apt to shorten his road by cutting across a knoll instead of winding around it; and then the wheels are noiseless on the turf; the branches crash as the vehicle is forced between the trees; and the wood-pigeons, frightened from their roost, flutter abroad. . . .

Our stationary rural life in the South was various and pleasant enough; all shaded with the presence of Slavery, but without any other drawback. There is something in the make-shift, irregular mode of life which exists where there are slaves, that is amusing when the cause is forgotten.

The waking in the morning is accomplished by two or three black women staring at you from the bed-posts. Then it is five minutes' work to get them out of the room. Perhaps, before you are half dressed, you are summoned to breakfast. You look at your watch, and listen whether it has stopped, for it seems not to be seven o'clock yet. You hasten, however, and find your hostess making the coffee. The young people drop in when the meal is half done, and then it is discovered that breakfast has been served an hour too early, because the clock has stopped, and the cook has ordered affairs according to her own conjectures. Everybody laughs, and nothing ensues. After breakfast a farmer in homespun—blue trousers and an orange-brown coat, or all over gray—comes to speak with your host. A drunken white has shot one of his

---

[5] **superintending**—overseeing; directing.

negroes, and he fears no punishment can be obtained, because there were no witnesses of the deed but blacks. A consultation is held whether the affair shall go into court; and, before the farmer departs, he is offered cake and liqueur.

Your hostess, meantime, has given her orders, and is now engaged in a back room, or out in the piazza behind the house, cutting out clothes for her slaves; very laborious work in warm weather. There may be a pretense of lessons among the young people, and something more than pretense if they happen to have a tutor or governess; but the probability is that their occupations are as various as their tempers. Rosa cannot be found; she is lying on the bed in her own room reading a novel; Clara is weeping for her canary, which has flown away while she was playing with it; Alfred is trying to ascertain how soon we may all go out to ride; and the little ones are lounging about the court, with their arms round the necks of blacks of their own size. You sit down to the piano or to read, and one slave or another enters every half hour to ask what is o'clock. Your hostess comes in at length, and you sit down to work with her; she gratifies your curiosity about her people, telling you how soon they burn out their shoes at the toes, and wear out their winter woollens, and tear up their summer cottons; and how impossible it is to get black women to learn to cut out clothes without waste; and how she never inquires when and where the whipping is done, as it is the overseer's business, and not hers. She has not been seated many minutes when she is called away, and returns saying how babyish these people are, that they will not take medicine unless she gives it to them; and how careless of each other, so that she has been obliged to stand by and see Diana put clean linen upon her infant, and to compel Bet to get her sick husband some breakfast. . . .

[On another plantation you are] taken to the cotton-gin, the building to your left, where you are shown how the cotton, as picked from the pods, is drawn between cylinders so as to leave the seeds behind; and how it is afterward packed, by hard pressure, into bales. The neighboring creek is dammed up to supply the water-wheel by which this gin is worked. You afterward see the cotton-seed laid in handfuls round the stalks of the young springing corn, and used in the cotton field as manure.

Meantime you attempt to talk with the slaves. You ask how old that very aged man is, or that boy; they will give you no **intelligible**[6] answer. Slaves never know, or never will tell, their ages, and this is the reason why the census presents such extraordinary reports on this point, declaring a great number to be above a hundred years old. If they have a kind master, they will boast to you of how much he gave for each of them, and what sums he has refused for them. If they have a hard master, they will tell you that they would have more to eat and be less flogged, but that massa is busy, and has no time to come down and see that they have enough to eat. Your hostess is well known on this plantation, and her kind face has been recognized from a distance; and already a negro woman has come to her with seven or eight eggs, for which she knows she shall receive a quarter dollar. You follow her to the negro quarter, where you see a tidy woman knitting, while the little children who are left in her charge are basking in the sun, or playing all kinds of antics in the road; little shining, plump, cleareyed children, whose mirth makes you sad when you look round upon their

---

[6] **intelligible**—understandable.

parents, and see what these bright creatures are to come to. You enter one of the dwellings, where everything seems to be of the same dusky hue: the crib against the wall, the walls themselves, and the floor, all look one yellow. More children are crouched round the wood fire, lying almost in the embers. You see a woman pressing up against the wall like an idiot, with her shoulder turned towards you, and her apron held up to her face. You ask what is the matter with her, and are told that she is shy. You see a woman rolling herself about in a crib, with her head tied up. You ask if she is ill, and are told that she has not a good temper; that she struck at a girl she was jealous of with an axe, and the weapon being taken from her, she threw herself into the well, and was nearly drowned before she was taken out, with her head much hurt.

The overseer has, meantime, been telling your host about the fever having been more or less severe last season, and how well off he shall think himself if he has no more than so many days' illness this summer: how the vegetation has suffered from the late frosts, pointing out how many of the oranges have been cut off, but that the great magnolia in the center of the court is safe. You are then invited to see the house, learning by the way the extent and value of the estate you are visiting, and of the "force" upon it. You admire the lofty, cool rooms, with their green blinds, and the width of the piazzas on both sides of the house, built to compensate for the want of shade from trees, which cannot be allowed near the dwelling for fear of mosquitos. You visit the icehouse, and find it pretty full, the last winter having been a severe one. You learn that, for three or four seasons after this icehouse was built, there was not a spike of ice in the state, and a cargo had to be imported from Massachusetts.

When you have walked in the field as long as the heat will allow, you step into the overseer's bare dwelling, within its bare enclosure, where fowls are strutting about, and fresh yourself with a small tumbler of milk; a great luxury, which has been ordered for the party. The overseer's fishing-tackle and rifle are on the wall, and there is a medicine chest and a shelf of books. He is tall, **sallow,**[7] and nonchalant, dropping nothing more about himself and his situation than that he does not know that he has had more than his share of sickness and much trouble in his vocation, and so he is pretty well satisfied.

---

[7] **sallow**—having a yellowish complexion.

QUESTIONS TO CONSIDER

1. How would you describe Martineau's tone and and attitude toward plantation life?

2. Why does the mirth of the slave children sadden Martineau?

3. Based on Martineau's observations, what type of relationship appears to exist between the slaves and the plantation owner's wife?

Slave Life

BY FREDERICK DOUGLASS

The great champion of civil rights, Frederick Douglass, was born a slave in Tuckahoe, Maryland, in 1818. In spite of laws forbidding slaves to read and write, he taught himself in childhood. An outstanding public speaker, he was active in the abolitionist movement. During the Civil War he worked to make black men eligible for military service in the Union forces. Two of his sons fought in the war. After the war, he continued to speak out on matters of discrimination. This selection is from the Narrative of the Life of Frederick Douglass, An American Slave, Written by Himself, *which was first published in 1845 by the Anti-Slavery Office in Boston. Here Douglass describes the plantation on which he was born, what life was like for the slaves, and why they almost always said they were contented and that their masters were kind.*

Colonel Lloyd kept from three to four hundred slaves on his home plantation, and owned a large number more on the neighboring farms belonging to him. The names of the farms nearest to the home plantation were Wye Town and New Design. "Wye Town" was under the overseership of a man named Noah Willis. New Design was under the overseership of a Mr. Townsend. The overseers of these, and all the rest of the farms, numbering over twenty, received advice and direction from the managers of the home plantation. This was the great business place. It was the seat of government for the whole twenty farms. All disputes among the overseers were settled here. If a slave was convicted of any high misdemeanor, became unmanageable, or evinced a determination to run away, he was brought immediately here, severely whipped, put on board the sloop,[1] carried to Baltimore, and sold to Austin Woolfolk, or some other slave-trader, as a warning to the slaves remaining.

Here, too, the slaves of all the other farms received their monthly allowance of food, and their yearly clothing. The men and women slaves received, as their monthly allowance of food, eight pounds of pork, or its equivalent in fish, and one bushel of corn meal. Their yearly clothing consisted of two coarse linen shirts, one pair of linen trousers, like the shirts, one jacket, one pair of trousers for winter, made of coarse negro cloth, one pair of stockings, and one pair of shoes; the whole of which could not have cost more than seven dollars. The allowance of the slave children was given to their mothers, or the old women having the care of them. The children unable to work in the field had neither shoes, stockings, jackets, nor trousers, given to them; their clothing consisted of two coarse linen shirts per year. When these failed them, they went naked until the next allowance-day. Children from seven to ten years old, of both sexes, almost naked, might be seen at all seasons of the year.

There were no beds given the slaves, unless one coarse blanket be considered such, and none but the

---

[1] sloop—sailing ship; sailboat.

men and women had these. This, however, is not considered a very great **privation**.[2] They find less difficulty from the want of beds, than from the want of time to sleep; for when their day's work in the field is done, the most of them having their washing, mending, and cooking to do, and having few or none of the ordinary facilities for doing either of these, very many of their sleeping hours are consumed in preparing for the field the coming day; and when this is done, old and young, male and female, married and single, drop down side by side, on one common bed,—the cold, damp floor,—each covering himself or herself with their miserable blankets; and here they sleep till they are summoned to the field by the driver's horn. At the sound of this, all must rise, and be off to the field. There must be no halting; every one must be at his or her post; and woe betides them who hear not this morning summons to the field; for if they are not awakened by the sense of hearing, they are by the sense of feeling: no age nor sex finds any favor. Mr. Severe, the overseer, used to stand by the door of the quarter, armed with a large hickory stick and heavy cowskin, ready to whip any one who was so unfortunate as not to hear, or, from any other cause, was prevented from being ready to start for the field at the sound of the horn.

Mr. Severe was rightly named: he was a cruel man. I have seen him whip a woman, causing the blood to run half an hour at the time; and this, too, in the midst of her crying children, pleading for their mother's release. He seemed to take pleasure in manifesting his fiendish **barbarity**.[3] Added to his cruelty, he was a profane swearer. It was enough to chill the blood and stiffen the hair of an ordinary man to hear him talk. Scarce a sentence escaped him but that was commenced

---

[2] **privation**—a state of being deprived; a lack of what is needed for existence.

[3] **barbarity**—cruelty.

or concluded by some horrid oath. The field was the place to witness his cruelty and profanity. His presence made it both the field of blood and of blasphemy. From the rising till the going down of the sun, he was cursing, raving, cutting, and slashing among the slaves of the field, in the most frightful manner. His career was short. He died very soon after I went to Colonel Lloyd's; and he died as he lived, uttering, with his dying groans, bitter curses and horrid oaths. His death was regarded by the slaves as the result of merciful providence.

Mr. Severe's place was filled by a Mr. Hopkins. He was a very different man. He was less cruel, less profane, and made less noise, than Mr. Severe. His course was characterized by no extraordinary demonstrations of cruelty. He whipped, but seemed to take no pleasure in it. He was called by the slaves a good overseer.

The home plantation of Colonel Lloyd wore the appearance of a country village. All the mechanical operations for all the farms were performed here. The shoemaking and mending, the blacksmithing, cartwrighting,[4] coopering,[5] weaving, and grain-grinding, were all performed by the slaves on the home planta-tion. The whole place wore a business-like aspect very unlike the neighboring farms. The number of houses, too, conspired to give it advantage over the neighboring farms. It was called by the slaves the *Great House Farm.* Few privileges were esteemed higher by the slaves of the out-farms, than that of being selected to do errands at the Great House Farm. It was associated in their minds with greatness. A representative could not be prouder of his election to a seat in the American Congress, than a slave on one of the out-farms would be of his election to do errands at the Great House Farm. They regarded it as evidence of great confidence reposed in them by their overseers; and it was on this

---

[4] cartwrighting—making and repairing carts.

[5] coopering—barrel-making.

account, as well as a constant desire to be out of the field from under the driver's lash, that they esteemed it a high privilege, one worth careful living for. He was called the smartest and most trusty fellow, who had this honor conferred upon him the most frequently. The competitors for this office sought as diligently to please their overseers, as the office-seekers in the political parties seek to please and deceive the people. The same traits of character might be seen in Colonel Lloyd's slaves, as are seen in the slaves of the political parties.

The slaves selected to go to the Great House Farm, for the monthly allowance for themselves and their fellow-slaves, were peculiarly enthusiastic. While on their way, they would make the dense old woods, for miles around, reverberate with their wild songs, revealing at once the highest joy and the deepest sadness. They would compose and sing as they went along, consulting neither time nor tune. The thought that came up, came out—if not in the word, in the sound;—and as frequently in the one as in the other. They would sometimes sing the most pathetic sentiment in the most rapturous tone, and the most rapturous sentiment in the most pathetic tone. Into all of their songs they would manage to weave something of the Great House Farm. Especially would they do this, when leaving home. They would then sing most exultingly the following words:—

"I am going away to the Great House Farm!
O, yea! O, yea! O!"

This they would sing, as a chorus, to words which to many would seem unmeaning jargon, but which, nevertheless, were full of meaning to themselves. I have sometimes thought that the mere hearing of those songs would do more to impress some minds with the horrible character of slavery, than the reading of whole volumes of philosophy on the subject could do.

I did not, when a slave, understand the deep meaning of those rude and apparently incoherent songs. I was myself within the circle; so that I neither saw nor heard as those without might see and hear. They told a tale of woe which was then altogether beyond my feeble comprehension; they were tones loud, long, and deep; they breathed the prayer and complaint of souls boiling over with the bitterest anguish. Every tone was a testimony against slavery, and a prayer to God for deliverance from chains. The hearing of those wild notes always depressed my spirit, and filled me with ineffable sadness. I have frequently found myself in tears while hearing them. The mere recurrence to those songs, even now, afflicts me; and while I am writing these lines, an expression of feeling has already found its way down my cheek. To those songs I trace my first glimmering conception of the dehumanizing character of slavery. I can never get rid of that conception. Those songs still follow me, to deepen my hatred of slavery, and quicken my sympathies for my brethren in bonds. If any one wishes to be impressed with the soul-killing effects of slavery, let him go to Colonel Lloyd's plantation, and, on allowance-day, place himself in the deep pine woods, and there let him, in silence, analyze the sounds that shall pass through the chambers of his soul,—and if he is not thus impressed, it will only be because "there is no flesh in his **obdurate**[6] heart."

I have often been utterly astonished, since I came to the north, to find persons who could speak of the singing, among slaves, as evidence of their contentment and happiness. It is impossible to conceive of a greater mistake. Slaves sing most when they are most unhappy. The songs of the slave represent the sorrows of his heart; and he is relieved by them, only as an aching heart is relieved by its tears. At least, such is my experience.

---

[6] **obdurate**—hardened in wrongdoing or wickedness; hardhearted.

I have often sung to drown my sorrow, but seldom to express my happiness. Crying for joy, and singing for joy, were alike uncommon to me while in the jaws of slavery. The singing of a man cast away upon a desolate island might be as appropriately considered as evidence of contentment and happiness, as the singing of a slave; the songs of the one and of the other are prompted by the same emotion. . . .

To describe the wealth of Colonel Lloyd would be almost equal to describing the riches of Job.[7] He kept from ten to fifteen house-servants. He was said to own a thousand slaves, and I think this estimate quite within the truth. Colonel Lloyd owned so many that he did not know them when he saw them; nor did all the slaves of the out-farms know him. It is reported of him, that, while riding along the road one day, he met a colored man, and addressed him in the usual manner of speaking to colored people on the public highways of the south: "Well, boy, whom do you belong to?" "To Colonel Lloyd," replied the slave. "Well, does the colonel treat you well?" "No, sir," was the ready reply. "What, does he work you too hard?" "Yes, sir." "Well, don't he give you enough to eat?" "Yes, sir, he gives me enough, such as it is."

The colonel, after **ascertaining**[8] where the slave belonged, rode on; the man also went on about his business, not dreaming that he had been conversing with his master. He thought, said, and heard nothing more of the matter, until two or three weeks afterwards. The poor man was then informed by his overseer that, for having found fault with his master, he was now to be sold to a Georgia trader. He was immediately chained and handcuffed; and thus, without a moment's warning, he was

---

[7] Job—in the Bible, a righteous man who kept his faith in God throughout a series of calamities.

[8] **ascertaining**—discovering with certainty; finding out for sure.

snatched away, and forever **sundered,**[9] from his family and friends, by a hand more unrelenting than death. This is the penalty of telling the truth, of telling the simple truth, in answer to a series of plain questions.

It is partly in consequence of such facts, that slaves, when inquired of as to their condition and the character of their masters, almost universally say they are contented, and that their masters are kind. The slave-holders have been known to send in spies among their slaves, to ascertain their views and feelings in regard to their condition. The frequency of this has had the effect to establish among the slaves the **maxim,**[10] that a still tongue makes a wise head. They suppress the truth rather than take the consequences of telling it, and in so doing prove themselves a part of the human family. If they have any thing to say of their masters, it is generally in their masters' favor, especially when speaking to an untried man. I have been frequently asked, when a slave, if I had a kind master, and do not remember ever to have given a negative answer; nor did I, in pursuing this course, consider myself as uttering what was absolutely false; for I always measured the kindness of my master by the standard of kindness set up among slaveholders around us. Moreover, slaves are like other people, and imbibe prejudices quite common to others. They think their own better than that of others. Many, under the influence of this prejudice, think their own masters are better than the masters of other slaves; and this, too, in some cases, when the very reverse is true. Indeed, it is not uncommon for slaves even to fall out and quarrel among themselves about the relative goodness of their masters, each contending for the superior goodness of his own over that of the others.

---

[9] **sundered**—broken or wrenched apart; severed.

[10] **maxim**—a succinct way of expressing a fundamental principle, general truth, or rule of conduct.

At the very same time, they mutually **execrate**[11] their masters when viewed separately. It was so on our plantation. When Colonel Lloyd's slaves met the slaves of Jacob Jepson, they seldom parted without a quarrel about their masters; Colonel Lloyd's slaves contending that he was the richest, and Mr. Jepson's slaves that he was the smartest, and most of a man. Colonel Lloyd's slaves would boast his ability to buy and sell Jacob Jepson. Mr. Jepson's slaves would boast his ability to whip Colonel Lloyd. These quarrels would almost always end in a fight between the parties, and those that whipped were supposed to have gained the point at issue. They seemed to think that the greatness of their masters was transferable to themselves. It was considered as being bad enough to be a slave; but to be a poor man's slave was deemed a disgrace indeed!

---

[11] **execrate**—declare to be hateful or abhorrent; denounce.

QUESTIONS TO CONSIDER

1. Why was the maxim "a still tongue makes a wise head" particularly important to those held as slaves?

2. Why did some slaves compete with one another to see who had the richest or strongest master?

3. Douglass's tone is calm and even-tempered. Would his writing have been more or less effective had his tone been angry or sad? Why?

4. What point does Douglass want to make about slave songs?

Lucretia Mott Faces a Mob

BY MARGARET HOPE BEACON

The issues that led to the Civil War were not simple. Slavery certainly was a key issue. However, there were Southerners who hated slavery, and there were Northerners who hated abolitionists. Among the Northerners who worked to fight slavery were women's rights organizer Lucretia Mott and her husband James. They were Quakers. This selection, from an article about Lucretia Mott published in Quaker History, *provides a dramatic example of how unpopular abolitionists became and how brave Lucretia Mott could be.*

When the American Anti-Slavery Society was formed in Philadelphia in 1833 [the Motts] were pleased that the constitution pledged its members to work against slavery by moral means alone. The Philadelphia Female Anti-Slavery Society, organized by Lucretia and others four days later, echoed these sentiments. The

Motts supported their friend and fellow abolitionist William Lloyd Garrison as he began to unfold his commitment to nonresistance[1] in his paper *The Liberator*. And they supported another friend, Henry C. Wright, also an early advocate of turning the other cheek.

The Motts themselves had been for some time involved in the Free Produce movement: an effort to permit those who felt conscientious scruples against buying products grown by slave labor to obtain them in small Free Produce shops. The supporters of Free Produce did not explicitly see their movement as a form of boycott, or an effort to place the burden or moral **suasion**[2] on the merchant of slave-made produce, as it would have been seen in 20th-century nonviolent theory, but rather as answering a Christian need to keep oneself free of **complicity**.[3] James Mott ran such a shop in 1829, himself in transition from the trade of cotton merchant to that of wool merchant. He was also president of the Free Produce Society. Lucretia supported him in these moves, and she used free produce religiously. She often exhorted others to do the same, as at the 1837 Anti-Slavery Convention of American Women, when she introduced a resolution.

> That the support of the **iniquitous**[4] system of slavery at the South is dependent on the co-operation of the North, by commerce and manufactures, as well as by the consumption of its products—therefore that, despising the gain of oppression we recommend to our friends, by a candid and prayerful examination of the subject, to ascertain if it be not a duty to cleanse our

---

[1] nonresistance—the practice of refusing to resort to force, even in defense against violence.

[2] **suasion**—persuasion.

[3] **complicity**—involvement in a questionable act or crime.

[4] **iniquitous**—grossly unjust, evil.

hands from this unrighteous participation, by no longer indulging in the luxuries which come through this polluted channel; and in the supply of the necessary articles of food and clothing, &., that we "provide things honest in the sight of all men," by giving preference to goods which come through **requited**[5] labor.

In addition, Lucretia Mott began advocating non-resistance explicitly. In November of 1837 when an abolitionist editor in Alton, Illinois, Elijah Lovejoy, defended his presses by force when he was attacked by a proslavery mob, and was himself shot and killed, abolitionists were divided between those who viewed his action as heroic, and those who considered his resort to the use of force as weakening the moral principles of their position. Lucretia Mott felt the latter rather strongly. The Philadelphia Female Anti-Slavery Society, under her leadership, decided to hold a public meeting for the support of Lovejoy's widow, but stated that they regretted that he took up arms, not "the proper means" to pursue the antislavery crusade.

At first antislavery sentiment was respectable in the North. In Philadelphia, a number of prominent citizens had joined to form in 1775 the Pennsylvania Society for Promoting the Abolition of Slavery; the Relief of Negroes Unlawfully Held in Bondage; and For Improving the Condition of the African Race. Reorganized in 1784, it lobbied diligently to persuade the infant Congress to ban slavery. But as the years passed and slavery became more deeply entrenched in the South after the invention of the cotton gin, Northern businessmen began to feel that the antislavery movement was a danger, threatening to interrupt business connections up and down the Eastern seaboard, while Northern white laborers, especially the

---

[5] **requited**—paid.

newly arrived Irish immigrants, saw free black labor as possible competition for jobs. Antislavery spokespersons were frequently booed by angry mobs, and even the churches began to refuse the use of their buildings for antislavery meetings. Although the Society of Friends had a traditional concern against slavery, even the Quakers began to fear the **secular**[6] antislavery movement as disruptive, and to bar such gatherings in the meeting houses.

After several years of frustration, the reformers in Philadelphia decided to raise money for a structure of their own in which to hold antislavery and related meetings. By selling shares at twenty dollars apiece to some 2000 sympathetic persons, they were able to raise a sum of $40,000. Both James and Lucretia Mott started working on fundraising in 1836. In the early months of 1838 a beautiful new building, Pennsylvania Hall, began to take shape on Sixth Street between Mulberry and Sassafras. It had the pillared facade of a Greek temple. Its first floor contained a small auditorium, committee rooms, and a free produce store; the second floor consisted of a large hall with galleries. The whole was lit with modern gas, and there were ventilators in the ceiling to permit a flow of fresh air, all new inventions. By early May it was ready for use.

The dedication ceremonies were set for May 14. There were many speeches and a special poem written by John Greenleaf Whittier for the occasion. On Tuesday the 15th, the Second Annual Meeting of the Anti-Slavery Convention of American Women opened its sessions in the new hall. The women agreed upon resolutions calling for the boycotting of slave produce and for an end to slavery in the District of Columbia. They could not, however, agree on the question of the right or duty of antislavery women to speak to mixed or **promiscuous**[7]

---

[6] **secular**—non-church, non-religious.

[7] **promiscuous**—composed of all sorts of persons, for example, men and women; blacks and whites.

audiences. This issue, which had been brought to the fore by the speaking tour of Angelina and Sarah Grimke, was proving divisive in the Boston Female Anti-Slavery Society, where some women attached to Garrison, under the leadership of Maria Weston Chapman and her sisters, Caroline, Anne and Deborah Weston, were in favor of "promiscuous" speaking, and others, influenced by the more conservative, clerical wing of the movement, were opposed. Many of the New York women were close to the clerical wing and therefore also opposed antislavery women speaking to mixed audiences, while the Philadelphia Female Antislavery Society . . . supported public speaking for women. It was finally decided that a meeting would be held on Wednesday evening not under the formal sponsorship of the Convention, at which those who believed in woman's duty to speak to a mixed audience might be heard.

A mob had formed around the Hall on May 14, and each day it had become larger and uglier. When it was discovered that blacks and whites, men and women, were going to meet together at the hall, public prejudice against racial **"amalgamation"**[8] flared. Each day the crowd grew a little more threatening, and the feminist-abolitionists had to learn to walk through it, heads held high, in order to attend their meetings.

Word about the promiscuous meeting on Wednesday night had gotten out, and the mob which gathered was larger and uglier than at any time before. Much of the anger was directed against the black delegates. It was estimated that 10,000 persons, primarily men, sur-rounded Pennsylvania Hall, and threats to break in and stop proceedings were widespread. The few policemen present made no secret that their sympathies lay with the mob and made no effort to restrain it. When William Lloyd Garrison, the very symbol of antislavery, rose to

---

[8] **amalgamation**—mixture.

speak, some of the men surged into the hall, shouting catcalls.[9] Unperturbed, Maria Chapman made a ten-minute speech, followed by Angelina Grimke Weld. The day before, Grimke had married abolitionist Theodore Weld in a ceremony in which they pledged themselves to equality in marriage, and had asked black friends as well as white to witness their union. Word of this affair, with its aspect of "social amalgamation," had spread through the city and led to further fury. When Angelina Weld spoke, telling of her first-hand experience with slavery as a Southerner, the mob began to shout again and to throw brickbats.[10] This incensed a young admirer, Abby Kelley of Worcester, Massachusetts, who made an impassioned maiden speech as an antislavery orator. Lucretia Mott closed the meeting, deploring the fact that the session had not been sponsored by the convention. "Let us hope that such false notions of delicacy and propriety will not long obtain in this enlightened country," she said.

That night someone posted notices in prominent places throughout Philadelphia, calling on all citizens with a due regard for property and the preservation of the Constitution to interfere "forcibly if they must," with the proceedings of the convention. The crowd that gathered Thursday outside the hall was huge and in an ugly mood. Daniel Neall, the president of Pennsylvania Hall, visited the mayor with a delegation and asked for protection. The mayor told them that the trouble was their own fault for holding an amalgamated convention in the first place. Unable to protect the delegates, Daniel Neall next asked Lucretia Mott to suggest that the black women stay away, since they seemed to be the most exposed to danger. Mott agreed to deliver the message Thursday afternoon, but said that she did not agree with it, and hoped that no one would act upon it, not be put off by a "little *appearance* of danger."

---

[9] catcalls—rude remarks.

[10] brickbats—bits of brick, rocks.

Undeterred, the delegates of the convention completed their regular business sessions throughout the day. When it was time to adjourn, the women went arm in arm, each white delegate protecting a black woman, maintaining their dignity despite the outrageous words shouted and stones thrown by the mob. This technique, which had first been tried in Boston, again worked, and with no armor other than their own sense of moral purpose the women passed through the angry mob unharmed.

As soon as the hall was emptied, the mayor stepped forward and locked the door, then made a speech in which he told the mob that they must serve as his police. As for himself, he proposed to go home. After he had left, members of the mob burst the doors down, collected all the books and benches, and started a huge fire, breaking the gas pipes to increase the **conflagration**.[11] After a while fire companies arrived and played their hoses on the adjacent buildings, while the new hall burned to the ground.

William Lloyd Garrison, Maria Chapman and Anne Weston were staying at the Motts' house at 148 North Ninth Street, a few blocks from Pennsylvania Hall. When friends came by to report that the mob might attack the Motts' house after the hall was consumed, these visitors thought it prudent to leave town. Local abolitionists however gathered at the Motts, who themselves had decided that nonresistance principles demanded that they not flee. One friend moved some furniture and clothes to a neighbor's, while another volunteered to spend the evening next door at the home of Maria Davis, where two younger Mott daughters as well as Lucretia's mother, Anna Coffin, had taken refuge.

At the Mott house, Lucretia and James and their guests tried to talk as though nothing was happening, while young Thomas Mott ran in and out to find out

---

[11] **conflagration**—a large, destructive fire.

what was going on. By nine o'clock they learned that Pennsylvania Hall was consumed, and shortly afterwards, that a leader of the mob had shouted "On to the Motts" and started up Race Street toward the house on Ninth. But a friend of the Motts intervened. Shouting "On to the Motts" he turned the mob south, not north at the corner of Ninth and Race. Their anger unquenched, the members of the mob next attacked and burned Mother Bethel Church, then the nearby Shelter for Colored Orphans.

Undeterred by the burning of Pennsylvania Hall, the feminist-abolitionists met the next morning at the school house of Sarah Pugh to complete their convention, condemned the brutal actions of racial violence, and pledged themselves to "expand, not contract their social relations with their colored friends. . . ."

QUESTIONS TO CONSIDER

1. What does the general public's opinion of the abolitionists seem to be?

2. Were you surprised by Mott's claim that slavery of the South was "dependent on the cooperation of the North"? Explain.

3, Compare and contrast the Free Produce movement to a contemporary boycott of foods or services—one that you've read about in the newspapers or heard about on TV. What are some similarities and differences?

Abolitionists

Lucretia Mott (1793–1880) Best known as one of the founding organizers of the women's rights movement, reformer Lucretia Mott was a teacher, a Quaker minister, an abolitionist, and a peace activist. After the Fugitive Slave Act of 1850, she and her husband James, also a teacher, made their home a safe place for runaway slaves.

▲

Sojourner Truth (1797–1883) Truth was an evangelist, a reformer, an abolitionist, and a women's rights activist. She had been born a slave and was freed in 1843. At the beginning of the Civil War, she helped to gather supplies for volunteer African-American regiments. In 1864, she went to Washington, D. C., and helped integrate the streetcars there. President Abraham Lincoln received her. Later she was appointed to the National Freedmen's Relief Association and counseled former slaves in such matters as how to resettle and make a living.

▲

Harriet Tubman (1820–1913) Known as the "Moses of her people," Tubman was the grand conductor of the Underground Railroad. She led over 300 people to freedom. In the Civil War she served as a nurse, laundress, and spy to the Federal forces in coastal South Carolina.

▲

Frederick Douglass (1817–1895) Douglass was the preeminent
human rights leader of the 19th century. A great orator and writer, he
wrote his autobiography to answer charges that he was too well spoken
to have ever been a slave. In the Civil War, he was a consultant to
President Lincoln. He advised him to permit former slaves to serve in
the Army, and he advocated making slavery the key issue for the war.

▲

Harriet Beecher Stowe (1811–1896) The daughter of a
Congregational minister, Stowe was a teacher, writer, and
philanthropist. *Uncle Tom's Cabin,* which she wrote after learning
about the plight of slaves from friends and from visits to the
South, became immensely popular. It was translated into twenty-
three languages, and the play produced from it had standing-
room-only audiences.

The Underground Railroad

BY R. C. SMEDLEY, M.D.

Dr. Smedley wrote a History of the Underground Railroad in Chester and the Neighboring Counties of Pennsylvania *to preserve the stories of the abolitionists, most of them Quakers, who helped escaping slaves on their way to freedom. This selection is from the chapter on Isaac and Dinah Mendenhall, who ran a "station" on the railroad. Smedley describes the work of the famous Underground Railroad "conductor," Harriet Tubman, whose "passengers" often went by way of the Mendenhalls.*

ISAAC AND DINAH MENDENHALL

The home of Isaac and Dinah Mendenhall, in Kennett township [Pennsylvania] near Longwood, ten miles from Wilmington, was always open to receive the liberty-seeking slave. Their station being nearest the Delaware line was eagerly sought by fugitives as soon as they entered the Free State. They were generally sent by Thomas Garrett, of Wilmington, who, starting them on the road, directed them to "go on and on until they came to a stone-gate post, and then turn in." Sometimes he sent a note by them saying, "I send you three," (or four or five, as they might be) "bales of black wool," which was to assure them that these colored persons were not impostors.

No record was kept of the number they aided, but during a period of thirty-four years it amounted to several hundred. Many were well dressed and intelligent.

At one time fourteen came on a Seventh-day (Saturday) night and remained over next day. The women and children were secreted in a room in the spring-house, and the men in the barn. As they usually entertained a great many visitors on First-days (Sundays), and some of these were pro-slavery **Friends**,[1] the fugitives had to be kept very quiet. . . .

One woman whom Thomas Garrett brought there was a somewhat curious, but interesting character, and endowed with a spiritualistic faith. The first night after leaving her master she began to regret and to wonder whether or not she was doing right; whether she should return or continue her course and risk being captured and taken back. She went into a woods, and sat down and cried. While in that deep, prayerful spirit, as to what was best for her to do, a voice seemed to say to her, "Cheer up, Mary; go on, I will protect thee." With this fresh cheer in her heart, she went on, arrived at Thomas Garrett's, who, as above related, took her to Isaac Mendenhall's, where she remained three months, and was a most faithful servant. She said they were told in the South that "abolitionists were wicked people," but that "she never knowed there was such kind people in the world as they."

---

[1] **Friends**—members of the Society of Friends; Quakers.

HARRIET TUBMAN

A colored woman named Harriet Tubman, living near the line, was active in helping hundreds to escape. In point of bravery and success she might well be called a second Joan of Arc. She would go fearlessly into the Slave States, talk with the slaves, tell them how to escape, direct them on the road, and thus during one visit among them, would start numbers on their way northward to freedom. Large sums of money were offered for her capture, but all in vain. She could elude patrols and pursuers with as much ease and unconcern as an eagle would soar through the heavens. She "had faith in God;" always asked Him what to do, and to direct her, "which," she said, "He always did." She would talk about "consulting with God," or "asking of Him," just as one would consult a friend upon matters of business; and she said "He never deceived her."

After escaping from bondage herself, she set about devising means by which she could assist others in leaving. In her first effort she brought away her brother, with his wife and several children. Next she helped her aged parents from Virginia to a comfortable home in Auburn, N.Y. And thus encouraged, she continued making these trips, at intervals, for several years. Many who escaped through her directions to Thomas Garrett were sent by him to Isaac Mendenhall.

When the war broke out, she felt, as she said, that "the good Lord had come down to deliver her people, and she must go and help Him." She went into Georgia and Florida, attached herself to the army, performed an incredible amount of labor as cook, laundress, and nurse, and still more as the leader of soldiers in scouting parties and raids. She seemed to know no fear, and scarcely ever fatigue. They called her their Moses. On account of the valuable services she rendered, several of the officers testified that she was entitled to a pension from the Government.

HARBORING FUGITIVES

After the Christiana riot,[2] James N. Taylor[3] brought Parker, Pinkney, and Johnson and one other whose name was not known, to Isaac Mendenhall's. When James returned, the hunters had been at his place in search of any colored people who might have fled to him from the vicinity of Christiana.

The four men slept in the barn at Isaac Mendenhall's at nights, but during the day they husked corn in the field, with all the appearance of regular farm hands. If pursuers came, the family were to give a certain sound when the men were to flee to the woods. One day a messenger came and said there was a party on the track of these men, and it would not be safe to keep them longer. During the remainder of the day they concealed themselves in the woods. Isaac decided to take them that night to John Vickers; but Dr. Bartholomew Fussell, then living near by, at Hamorton, hearing that the men were there, went to consult with him about them. Learning his decision, he said, "Isaac, I am better acquainted with the route than thee is; and beside, I have no property to sacrifice if I am detected, and thee has. Thee start with them on the road and I will meet thee and go on with them, and thee can return." After some deliberation, Isaac accepted the proposition, and at an appointed hour in the evening, started.

Dinah Mendenhall, in relating this case, said: "These men were not only fugitives but participants in the tragedy, and harboring them subjected us to heavy fine and imprisonment. But we had always said we would never submit to carry out that accursed Fugitive Slave Law, come what might. But that night when they started, the poor quivering flesh was weak and I had scarce

---

[2] Christiana riot—a major black revolt, which took place in 1851, against slave-catchers from Maryland.

[3] James Taylor is another, like Garrett, who helped direct the fugitives to safe homes.

strength to get into the house. But I held to my faith in an Overruling Providence, and we came through it in safety." "These," she remarked, "were the times which tried men's souls, and women's too."

Doctor Fussell, instead of taking them to John Vickers, took them to his niece, Graceanna Lewis, arriving there before midnight. Leaving them in the conveyance,[4] he went to the house, awoke the family, told them whom he had with him and what the danger would be in harboring them. They admitted them, however, and put them in a third-story room, the door of which locked on the inside. They were told not to unlock it unless a certain signal was given. As the girl then living with the family was not to be trusted, they borrowed food for the men from a neighbor, so as not to excite her suspicion. The following day arrangements were made with J. Pierce West, living near by, to take them to the house of a friend in Montgomery county, about a mile or more from Phoenixville. A little after dark he and his brother, Thomas, started with them in a market dearborn,[5] throwing some old carpet over them, just as they would cover a butter-tub. Passing through Phoenixville about midnight, they arrived at the friend's house, whose name is not now remembered, and there left them. . . .

PERSUADING OTHERS

Many families along these routes who were inherently opposed to slavery, refused, through fear, to give any assistance whatever in facilitating the fugitives' escape.

There were many persons in Kennett township who were not strenuously opposed to the anti-slavery movement; were inclined to be sympathizers in the cause, but thought abolitionists were running great risks.

---

[4] conveyance—cart or other vehicle of transportation.

[5] market dearborn—horse-drawn wagon.

Anti-slavery lectures in that township did much to enlighten the people upon universal liberty and to soften the **asperity**[6] of antagonism toward abolitionists, although many meetings, in the early part of the time, were but slimly attended.

Many persons in Kennett and vicinity grew to be conscientiously opposed to using the products of slave labor, as by so doing they were patronizing an evil that they were endeavoring to uproot. To meet the demand of these persons, Sarah Pearson opened a free produce store in Hamorton, about the year 1844, and continued it fourteen years. She was well patronized. At first she kept only free produce; but later kept mixed goods.

Kennett Monthly Meeting of Friends disowned several of its members who had, in a measure, separated themselves from it, on account of the meeting's not taking as active a part in anti-slavery, temperance, and other needed reforms of the day, as they held it to be the moral duty of a religious body to do. Isaac Mendenhall was one who came under this decree of disownment,[7] but his wife, as earnest in the progressive movement of reform as he, was never disowned. It is a principle of Friends to act in harmony. In the consideration of her case there was a "division of sentiment."

They united with a number of others in organizing the Society of Progressive Friends . . . [and] a large number of persons assembled in Old Kennett (Friends) Meeting House, on the twenty-second of Fifth month (May), 1853. The house was filled and many could not gain entrance. . . . The call to this Conference was signed by fifty-eight persons, chiefly Friends. Its sessions continued four days and were marked by free and cordial interchange of views, development of thought, and an earnestness and unity of action for the enlightenment,

---

[6] **asperity**—harshness or severity.

[7] After the war, the Kennett Monthly Meeting invited back the people they had disowned without requiring them to acknowledge wrongdoing.

improvement and general welfare of the whole human family. That aged and religious emancipated slave, Sojourner Truth, was there, and spoke on several occasions. She touched the sympathies of all, and reached the deep fount of parental tenderness, when, after a few impressive remarks, she sang:

> I pity the slave-mother, careworn and weary,
>> Who sighs as she presses her babe to her
>>> breast;
> I lament her sad fate, all so helpless and dreary,
>> I lament for her woes, and her wrongs
>>> unredressed.
> O! who can imagine her heart's deep emotion,
>> As she thinks of her children about to be
>>> sold;
> You may picture the bounds of the rock-girdled
>> ocean,
>> *But the grief of that mother can never*
>>> *be told.*

QUESTIONS TO CONSIDER

1. Why did the Friends decide to participate in the Abolitionist movement?

2. Were all Friends of the same mind when it came to the issue of slavery? Explain with examples.

3. What point was Sojourner Truth making when she compared the ocean to a slave-mother's grief?

Florida Passes the Ordinance of Secession

BY SUSAN BRADFORD

For some Southern leaders, the election of Abraham Lincoln as President in November 1860 meant there was no longer any choice but to secede. On December 20th, delegates elected by the people of South Carolina unanimously passed the Ordinance of Secession, declaring South Carolina a free and independent Republic. By February 1, 1861, Mississippi, Florida, Alabama, Georgia, Louisiana, and Texas had seceded also. In Katharine M. Jones's book, Heroines of Dixie: Confederate Women Tell Their Story of the War, *the author includes the diary entries of Susan Bradford, who was fourteen at the time. Like many Southerners, even Bradford's own family members hold strong differences of opinion.*

Pine Hill Plantation
Leon County, Florida

January 1, 1861—A New Year has come to us now. As we sat around the long table today the conversation turned on the convention, so soon to meet in Tallahassee. Father said he considered this the most momentous year in the history of the South. He is for Secession and he does not think that war will necessarily follow. Brother Junius is a strong Union man and he thinks we will certainly have war; he says we will have war in any event. If the South secedes the North will fight to keep us, and if we do not secede, all property rights will be taken from us and we will be obliged to fight to hold our own. He says he is for the fight but he wants to fight in the Union not out of it. Father thinks it is more honorable to take an open and decided stand and let all the world know what we are doing. Everyone at table who expressed an opinion was firmly set against the Republican party. Mother says she wants the negroes freed but she wants the United States Government to make laws which will free them gradually. All agree on one point, if the negroes are freed our lands will be worthless.

January 2, 1861—Uncle Richard and Uncle Tom spent the morning with Father, the three brothers are going to Tallahassee tomorrow to the opening of the Secession Convention.

January 3, 1861—I would not write this morning because I wanted to put down in my diary the first news of the convention. Tonight Father has told me what they did; it was simply to organize and then they adjourned. Some of the delegates had not arrived and this will give them the opportunity to get to Tallahassee and present their credentials. Father says the Capitol was full of men from all over the State and they look very serious.

January 4, 1861—I can hardly keep my mind on my books I am thinking so much of the probable action of the convention. I know Father must have been glad when the school bell rang this morning, it seems impossible for me to refrain from asking him questions, which, of course, must be troublesome.

January 5, 1861—This is Saturday and Mother lets Lula make candy on Saturday and if she, my black mammy, will let us, we help with it. Cousin Rob is spending the day here and Lula has promised to teach us how to make the candy baskets. Cousin Rob does not care about the convention, he is going to school in town but comes home Friday after school and goes back Monday morning.

January 6, 1861—This morning we went to Mount Zion to hear Mr. Blake preach. Today he spoke so earnestly of the representatives of the people of Florida, now in convention assembled in Tallahassee. He spoke of the heavy responsibility resting on them; of the high compliment paid them by the people of Florida, in trusting them with an issue of such paramount importance. He said we, none of us, knew which way was best; we must trust in God and do good.

Mr. Blake took dinner with us and Eddie came with him. He is just the shyest boy. When the company were all gone Father told me to ask Lula to get me ready to go with him to town next morning. He said he was going to show me what a convention was like. I was so happy at the thought of going and my heart fell when Mother said: "Surely, Dr. Bradford, you are not going to take the child away from school?" but Father said, "Yes, I am going to take her with me in the morning. This is history in the making, she will learn more than she can get out of books, and what she hears in this way she will never forget." I am so glad. I am so excited I cannot hold my pencil steady but I must write this down.

January 7, 1861—I am so glad it is not raining today. I am really going and, little diary, I will tell you all about the day when we get home.

8:30 P.M. We have just finished supper. Mother would not let me write until we had eaten, now she says I can only have one hour because I am going again tomorrow and must have a good sleep.

The convention was assembling in the hall of representatives when we entered the Capitol, and soon everybody was in place and Dr. DuBose made a very fine prayer.

After the preliminaries were disposed of a communication from the Governor was read and the first thing I knew Aunt Mary, who was sitting next, caught me by the hand and said, "Look, there is the ambassador from South Carolina." A small man very erect and slender was being introduced by Mr. Villepigue as Mr. Leonidas Spratt of South Carolina. Mr. Spratt bowed gravely and looking around upon the audience with a pair of brilliant, beautiful eyes, he began somewhat in this manner, though I probably will not get it quite right.

He said he felt some delicacy in appearing before this convention, coming as he did from a foreign power, but the heart of South Carolina was filled with love and sympathy for Florida, who now was standing where Carolina had so lately stood. Then he read aloud a communication from his state, recounting the grievances, which had led her to sever the ties which bound her to the Union. You never heard such cheers and shouts as rent the air, and it lasted so long. When quiet was restored Mr. Villepigue introduced Colonel Bulloch, of Alabama. He made a fine address but a short one. Said his own state was now deliberating as to what course she should pursue and had sent him to assure Florida of her cordial good-will. He sat down amid cheers for "Bulloch and Alabama."

Mr. Edmund Ruffin, of Virginia, was introduced and said he came to tell us that Virginia was with her Southern sisters in feeling and, if the worse came to the worst, she would be with them, heart and soul. He is a splendid looking man, quite old and yet he is perfectly erect and only his snow-white hair shows his age. He reminds me very much of dear Grandpa, who is taking such a warm interest in these proceedings, though he is so far away. I believe it will break his heart if North Carolina does not secede.

When the speaking was over and a few resolutions had been passed the convention adjourned and we came home. We left a noisy crowd behind us. As far as we could hear there were cheers for South Carolina; cheers for Mississippi; cheers for Alabama and for Florida. Never before have I seen such excitement. It even throws the horse races in the shade. What will tomorrow bring?

January 8, 1861—We are at home again after a day filled to overflowing with excitement and interest. We were in such a hurry to get to town that the convention had not assembled when we reached the Capitol. There were groups of men talking earnestly and there were other men running hither and thither with papers in their hands. Father has a great many friends and I stood quietly beside him while he and they discussed the situation. The ambassador from South Carolina had evidently made an impression on his audience of yesterday and somebody had been busy last night, for in every direction could be seen Palmetto cockades,[1] fastened with a blue ribbon; there were hundreds of them. When at last the hall of representatives was opened and Father and I took seats, Judge Gwynn came in and pinned a cockade on Father and one on me. Oh, I was so proud.

---

[1] Palmetto cockades—small ornaments, worn as badges, made from palmetto leaves.

The members of the convention took their seats and Mr. Blake, our dear Mr. Blake, whom we love so well, opened the day's session with prayer. I had never seen a convention until Father brought me here, and it is strange to me. I wish I could tell all I heard today, but the language the members used is not familiar to me and some of the things they talk about are just as new. Then, too, I am just a little girl. A message was read on the floor of the convention, from Governor Brown of Georgia, to Governor Milton. As near as I can remember it was this way: "Georgia will certainly secede. Has Florida occupied the fort?"

Mr. Sanderson was very interesting. He recounted the rights which the states retained when they delegated other rights to the general government in the Constitution. He made it so perfectly clear that all and every state had the right to withdraw from the Union, if her rights and liberty were threatened. He said the Committee on Ordinances had carefully examined into the question and they could find no reason why Florida should not exercise her right to withdraw from a compact, which now threatened her with such dire disaster. I am going again tomorrow. My palmetto cockade lies on the table beside me.

January 9, 1861—There has been a hot time in the convention today; the nearer they get to a final decision the hotter it gets. Colonel Ward made a most eloquent address to the convention. He told them that he was a Union man but it was in this way: in his opinion the South had done more to establish that Union than any other section; it was a Southern man who wrote the Declaration of Independence, it was a Southern man who led the American army, it was Southern men who framed the Constitution, a Southern man wrote our National Anthem and, in so doing, had immortalized the Star-spangled Banner and he proposed to hold on to that which we had done so much to bring about. He was willing to fight, if fight we must, but he wanted to fight in the Union and under that flag which was doubly ours. The heartiest applause greeted him as he sat down. It was plain to see that his audience was tremendously affected but the next speaker tore his fine argument to shreds. So it went on all day, some committee business would interrupt now and then but the most of the time was spent in debate for or against secession.

Our old friend, Mr. Burgess, says: "If Mrs. Harriet Beecher Stowe had died before she wrote 'Uncle Tom's Cabin,' this would never have happened." He says, "she has kindled a fire which all the waters of the earth cannot extinguish." Isn't it strange how much harm a pack of lies can do?

January 10, 1861—It is night and I am very tired but there is much to tell. The Ordinance of Secession was voted on today. Bishop Rutledge made the opening prayer and it was very impressive. He pleaded so earnestly for God's guidance for these members, in whose hands lay the future of Florida. These men feel their responsibility I am sure, their faces are so serious and yet so alert. I heard something today about a flag which had been presented to Florida, but I have not seen it yet.

After the committees were disposed of, the Ordinance of Secession was voted on. The vote was 62 for and 7 against. The ordinance was declared adopted at 22 minutes after 12 o'clock. It was resolved that at one o'clock on the next day, January 11th, the Ordinance of Secession should be signed on the east portico of the Capitol. The convention then adjourned until the afternoon session.

Mississippi seceded last night and it seems we will have plenty of company. The Union men in the hall looked very sad. They have worked hard for their side, but they had only a few followers.

January 11, 1861—We did not try to be early this morning, as the big event of the day did not take place until one o'clock. Capitol Square was so crowded you could see nothing but heads and the Capitol itself was full of people looking from the windows, which looked out on the east portico. Somehow Father and I had seats on the portico itself, close up to the wall where we were not in the way and yet we could both see and hear.

There was a table already there with a large ink-stand and several pens, nothing more. A subdued murmur came from the assembled citizens but there was none of the noise and excitement which had prevailed on other days; all seemed impressed with the solemnity of the occasion for oh, it is solemn! I did not realize how solemn until Mr. Sanderson read the Constitution and I understood just why it was necessary for Florida to secede.

As the old town clock struck one, the Convention, headed by President McGehee, walked out on the portico. In a few moments they were grouped about the table on which some one had spread the parchment on which the Ordinance of Secession was written. It was impossible for me to tell in what order it was signed, the heads were clustered so closely around the table, but presently I heard Col. Ward's familiar voice. There was a little break in the crowd and I saw him quite plainly. He dipped his pen in the ink and, holding it aloft, he said, in the saddest of tones, "When I die I want it inscribed upon my tombstone that I was the last man to give up the ship." Then he wrote slowly across the sheet before him, "George T. Ward."

The stillness could almost be felt. One by one they came forward.

When at length the names were all affixed, cheer after cheer rent the air; it was deafening. Our world seemed to have gone wild.

General Call is an old man now; and he is a strong Union man. Chancing to look toward him I saw that the tears were streaming down his face. Everybody cannot be suited and we are fairly launched on these new waters; may the voyage be a prosperous one.

Nearly everybody seems to be happy and satisfied. The Supreme Court Judges, into whose hands the document just signed has been placed, have carried it to Miss Elizabeth Eppes to engross or adorn it with blue ribbon; the judges selected Miss Bettie because she is a granddaughter of Thomas Jefferson. I hope President Jefferson likes our Ordinance—I believe those who are gone know all we are doing here below.

Father says the rest of the proceedings of this convention will be confined to business matters and though he is planning to attend, he will leave me at home and let me go on with my studies. I wonder if I can collect my wits enough to learn my lessons. I will have Saturday to rest up in and Lula will make us some candy. . . .

QUESTIONS TO CONSIDER

1. What is the position of the secessionists? What is the position of the unionists?

2. Why does Susan Bradford call *Uncle Tom's Cabin* a "pack of lies"?

3. What do the palmetto cockades symbolize for Susan and others at the convention?

CHAPTER 4

The War Day In
and Day Out

Soldier Life in the Army of Northern Virginia

BY CARLTON McCARTHY

The Confederacy was formed on February 4, 1861. On April 12, the Confederate forces fired the first shots of the war at Fort Sumter, outside Charleston, South Carolina. On April 17, Virginia seceded and joined the Confederacy. Private Carlton McCarthy, of the Army of Northern Virginia, wrote in the introduction to his book, "The Confederate soldier was a venerable old man, a youth, a child, a preacher, a farmer, merchant, student, statesman, orator, father, brother, husband, son—the wonder of the world, the terror of his foes!" Here he describes how these soldiers outfitted themselves to go to war—and then what happened.

The volunteer of 1861 made extensive preparations for the field. Boots, he thought, were an absolute necessity, and the heavier the soles and longer the tops the better. His pants were stuffed inside the tops of his boots, of course. A double-breasted coat, heavily wadded, with two rows of big brass buttons and a long skirt, was considered comfortable. A small stiff cap, with a narrow brim, took the place of the comfortable "felt," or the shining and towering tile worn in civil life.

Then over all was a huge overcoat, long and heavy, with a cape reaching nearly to the waist. On his back he strapped a knapsack containing a full stock of underwear, soap, towels, comb, brush, looking-glass, tooth-brush, paper and envelopes, pens, ink, pencils, blacking,[1] photographs, smoking and chewing tobacco, pipes, twine string, and cotton strips for wounds and other emergencies, needles and thread, buttons, knife, fork, and spoon, and many other things as each man's idea of what he was to encounter varied. On the outside of the knapsack, solidly folded, were two great blankets and a rubber or oil-cloth. This knapsack, etc., weighed from fifteen to twenty-five pounds, sometimes even more. All seemed to think it was impossible to have on too many or too heavy clothes, or to have too many conveniences, and each had an idea that to be a good soldier he must be provided against every possible emergency.

In addition to the knapsack, each man had a haver-sack,[2] more or less costly, some of cloth and some of fine morocco,[3] and stored with provisions always, as though he expected any moment to receive orders to march across the Great Desert, and supply his own wants on the way. A canteen was considered indispensable, and at the outset it was thought prudent to keep it full of water. Many, expecting terrific hand-to-hand encounters, carried revolvers, and even bowie-knives. Merino[4] shirts (and flannel) were thought to be the right thing, but

---

[1] blacking—black oil or polish for leather.
[2] haversack—bag carried over one shoulder to transport supplies.
[3] morocco—soft, fine leather of goatskin used for book bindings and shoes.
[4] merino—lightweight fabric made from the wool of merino sheep.

experience demonstrated the contrary. Gloves were also thought to be very necessary and good things to have in winter time, the favorite style being buck gauntlets with long cuffs.

In addition to each man's private luggage, each mess,[5] generally composed of from five to ten men, drawn together by similar tastes and associations, had its outfit, consisting of a large camp chest containing skillet, frying pan, coffee boiler, bucket for lard, coffee box, salt box, sugar box, meal box, flour box, knives, forks, spoons, plates, cups, etc., etc. These chests were so large that eight or ten of them filled up an army wagon, and were so heavy that two strong men had all they could do to get one of them into the wagon. In addition to the chest each mess owned an axe, water bucket, and bread tray. Then the tents of each company, and little sheet-iron stoves, and stove pipe, and the trunks and valises of the company officers, made an immense pile of stuff, so that each company had a small wagon train of its own.

All thought money to be absolutely necessary, and for awhile rations were disdained and the mess supplied with the best that could be bought with the mess fund. Quite a large number had a "boy" along to do the cooking and washing. Think of it! a Confederate soldier with a body servant all his own, to bring him a drink of water, black his boots, dust his clothes, cook his corn bread and bacon, and put wood on his fire. . . .

It is amusing to think of the follies of the early part of the war, as illustrated by the outfits of the volunteers. They were so heavily clad, and so burdened with all manner of things, that a march was torture, and the wagon trains were so immense in proportion to the number of troops, that it would have been impossible to guard them in an enemy's country. . . .

---

[5] mess—group of soldiers who eat together.

Thus much by way of introduction. The change came rapidly. . . . Experience soon demonstrated that boots were not agreeable on a long march. They were heavy and irksome, and when the heels were worn a little one-sided, the wearer would find his ankle twisted nearly out of joint by every unevenness of the road. When thoroughly wet, it was a laborious undertaking to get them off, and worse to get them on in time to answer the morning roll-call. And so, good, strong brogues or brogans, with broad bottoms and big, flat heels, succeeded the boots. . . .

A short-waisted and single-breasted jacket usurped the place of the long-tailed coat, and became universal. The enemy noticed this peculiarity, and called the Confederates "gray jackets."

Caps were destined to hold out longer than some other uncomfortable things, but they finally yielded to the demands of comfort and common sense, and a good soft felt hat was worn instead. A man who has never been a soldier does not know, nor indeed can know, the amount of comfort there is in a good soft hat in camp, and how utterly useless is a "soldier hat" as they are generally made. Why the Prussians, with all their experience, wear their heavy, unyielding helmets, and the French their little caps, is a mystery to a Confederate who has enjoyed the comfort of an old slouch.

Overcoats an inexperienced man would think an absolute necessity for men exposed to the rigors of a northern Virginia winter, but they grew scarcer and scarcer. . . . The men came to the conclusion that the trouble of carrying them on hot days outweighed the comfort of having them when the cold day arrived. Besides they found that life in the open air hardened them to such an extent that changes in the temperature were not felt to any degree. . . .

The knapsack vanished early in the struggle. It was inconvenient to "change" the underwear too often, and the disposition not to change grew, as the knapsack was found to gall the back and shoulders, and weary the man before half the march was accomplished. The better way was to dress out and out, and wear that outfit until the enemy's knapsacks, or the folks at home supplied a change. Certainly it did not pay to carry around clean clothes while waiting for the time to use them.

Very little washing was done, as a matter of course. Clothes once given up were parted with forever. There were good reasons for this: cold water would not cleanse them or destroy the vermin, and hot water was not always to be had. One blanket to each man was found to be as much as could be carried, and amply sufficient for the severest weather. This was carried generally by rolling it lengthwise, with the rubber cloth outside, tying the ends of the roll together, and throwing the loop thus made over the left shoulder with the ends fastened together hanging under the right arm.

The haversack held its own to the last, and was found practical and useful. It very seldom, however, contained rations, but was used to carry all the articles generally carried in the knapsack; of course the stock was small. Somehow or other, many men managed to do without the haversack, and carried absolutely nothing but what they wore and had in their pockets.

The infantry threw away their heavy cap boxes and cartridge boxes, and carried their caps and cartridges in their pockets. Canteens were very useful at times, but they were as a general thing discarded. . . . A good strong tin cup was found better than a canteen, as it was easier to fill at a well or spring, and was serviceable as a boiler for making coffee when the column halted for the night.

Revolvers were found to be about as useless and heavy lumber as a private soldier could carry, and early in the war were sent home to be used by the women and children in protecting themselves from insult and violence at the hands of the ruffians who prowled about the country shirking duty. . . .

Gloves to any but a mounted man were found useless, worse than useless. With the gloves on, it was impossible to handle an axe, buckle harness, load a musket, or handle a rammer at the piece. . . .

The camp chest soon vanished. The brigadiers and major-generals, even, found them too troublesome, and soon they were left entirely to the quartermasters[6] and commissaries. One skillet and a couple of frying pans, a bag for flour or meal, another bag for salt, sugar, and coffee, divided by a knot tied between, served the purpose as well. The skillet passed from mess to mess. Each mess generally owned a frying pan, but often one served a company. The oil-cloth was found to be as good as the wooden tray for making up the dough. The water bucket held its own to the last!

Tents were *rarely seen.* All the poetry about the *"tented field"* died. Two men slept together, each having a blanket and an oil-cloth; one oil-cloth went next to the ground. The two laid on this, covered themselves with two blankets, protected from the rain with the second oil-cloth on top, and slept very comfortably through rain, snow or hail, as it might be.

Very little money was seen in camp. The men did not expect, did not care for, or often get any pay, and they were not willing to deprive the old folks at home of their little supply, so they learned to do without any money.

When rations got short and were getting shorter, it became necessary to dismiss the servants. Some, however, became company servants, instead of private institutions, and held out faithfully to the end, cooking the rations away in the rear, and, at the risk of life, carrying them to the line of battle to their "young masters."

---

[6] quartermasters—officers responsible for the food, clothing, and equipment of troops.

Reduced to the minimum, the private soldier consisted of one man, one hat, one jacket, one shirt, one pair of pants, one pair of drawers, one pair of shoes, and one pair of socks. His baggage was one blanket, one rubber blanket, and one haversack. The haversack generally contained smoking tobacco and a pipe, and a small piece of soap, with temporary additions of apples, persimmons, blackberries, and such other commodities as he could pick up on the march.

The company property consisted of two or three skillets and frying pans, which were sometimes carried in the wagon, but oftener in the hands of the soldiers. The infantry-men generally preferred to stick the handle of the frying pan in the barrel of a musket, and so carry it.

The wagon trains were devoted entirely to the transportation of ammunition and **commissary**[7] and quartermaster's stores, which had not been issued. Rations which had become company property, and the baggage of the men, when they had any, was carried by the men themselves. If, as was sometimes the case, three days' rations were issued at one time and the troops ordered to cook them, and be prepared to march, they did cook them, *and eat them if possible,* so as to avoid the labor of carrying them. It was not such an undertaking either, to eat three days' rations in one, as frequently none had been issued for more than a day, and when issued were cut down one half.

The infantry found out that bayonets were not of much use, and did not hesitate to throw them, with the scabbard, away.

The artillerymen, who started out with heavy sabres hanging to their belts, stuck them up in the mud as they marched, and left them for the ordnance officers to pick up and turn over to the cavalry.

---

[7] **commissary**—food and cooking supplies.

The cavalrymen found sabres very tiresome when swung to the belt, and adopted the plan of fastening them to the saddle on the left side, with the hilt in front and in reach of the hand. Finally sabres got very scarce even among the cavalrymen, who relied more and more on their short rifles.

No soldiers ever marched with less to encumber them, and none marched faster or held out longer.

The courage and devotion of the men rose equal to every hardship and privation, and the very intensity of their sufferings became a source of merriment. Instead of growling and deserting, they laughed at their own bare feet, ragged clothes and pinched faces; and weak, hungry, cold, wet, worried with vermin and itch, dirty, with no hope of reward or rest, marched cheerfully to meet the well-fed and warmly clad hosts of the enemy.

QUESTIONS TO CONSIDER

1. Did the boys and men who enlisted in the Confederate Army understand what life as a soldier would be like? Find evidence from the text to support your opinion.

2. Do you think the author is critical or complimentary of Confederate soldiers? How do you know?

3. Which of the items ended up being useful to the Confederate volunteers? What distinguished these items from the others that were discarded?

Letters from a Sharpshooter

BY WILLIAM B. GREENE

Willie Greene had qualified to be a member of Hiram Berdan's Sharpshooters by putting ten consecutive shots in a ten-inch bull's-eye at 200 yards. He was only seventeen when he, along with many of his friends, signed up to join the Union Army. Being under 21, he should have had parental permission, but he didn't. When, at his request afterward, his mother wrote to try to get him discharged, she was told it was too late. He was to remain in the army for the entire war.

Washington
Jan. 3d 1862

Dear Mother,

I am alone tonight so I guess I will write to you. I received your last letter and money Jan. 1st as I told you in my other letter. You wanted me to tell you about

Frank Eastman. He did not know how he was going to be discharged so I thought I would wait until he heard from his folks. He got a letter today from his mother with $5.00 in it. She told him to keep still and not say anything about getting discharged but as he and I were pretty good friends he told me about it. He said that his folks got up a petition for a discharge and the governor of N.H. signed it and they sent it here for the Secretary of War to sign and if he signs it he is discharged. So if you can get some influential person to see the governor and tell him about my having the rheumatism then perhaps he will sign a petition for my discharge. Find out about it as soon as you get this.

This is the most sickly place I ever saw. I saw three men carted to the Soldiers' Home this afternoon and another that lay dead out of Co. B, a Michigan company. Our company has sick, this minute, nineteen men. There was two men carried to the hospital tonight and I should not be surprised if one of them died before tomorrow morning. There is two men sick out of my tent and we don't have much room. I don't feel very well tonight so I am going to tent with A.A. True.

One of the boys in my tent has the measles, the other the mumps. Have I ever had the mumps? I'll bet there is two hundred sick in this camp now and they have most of them got the measles. The mumps made their appearance in camp within a few days. I feel like helping them all I can. I have spent most all that money you sent me for cider and such stuff to drive the measles out of my companions.

There was a man came into camp today after a doctor. There was a shell blast in one of the Rhode Island regiments of cavalry that killed one man and wounded two more.

If you cannot do anything for me for my release I shall visit the Secretary of War myself. And if I cannot get discharged I suppose I shall have to remain. We get paid off in a few days. If I want any more money, I shall write to you again in a few days. Write as soon as you get this. Hazen Currier is waiting for a discharge. He has got a certificate from the doctor that he is not fit for a soldier.

Write as soon as you receive this. Send me a paper once in a while; the Union Democrat.

From your disobedient son,
W B G

Co. G 2nd Regiment
Berdan's Brigade U.S.S.S. [United States Sharp
    Shooters]
Camp of Instruction
Care of Capt. McPherson
Washington D. C.

Dear Mother,

I thought I would not write this on the other sheet. I want you to send me $20 as soon as you receive this. They have got the small pox over to the city and I don't have it. I am going to get a pass to go to the Fifth Regiment to be there two days and by the time the two days are out I shall be at home. Send as soon as you get this. Burn this up. I shall be at Raymond in a few days.

W B G

Raymond, Jan. 7th/62

My dear dear Willie,

How shall I write! What shall I say! Your letter has arrived containing such intelligence! You have experienced nothing more than I fully believed you would, but I could not make you believe it. It is no doubt very shocking for you to witness so much sickness & death. But it is unavoidable & you must try & be calm under it. One is twice as likely to be sick when they suffer themselves to be excited & feel afraid all of the time that they should be sick. The measles you will have no fear of for you have had them & the mumps I think you need not have much fear of them. I think you have had them light, by any rate you have been very much exposed to them a number of times & I think you need not have much fear on that ground. There is not much danger in having them unless one gets cold, if one would be very careful they would soon pass off. You say the small pox is in the city. I presume they have it there every winter. Some people think that it is not to be feared or dreaded as the measles are. When one has the small pox they have to keep quiet & cool as they can & live on gruel or something of that kind. You must live temperate & keep yourself clean. Take off your clothes often & air them and sponge yourself & rub briskly with one of your towels & be very careful about getting cold. When you bathe or sponge do it as quickly as possible. In regard to my petitioning to have you discharged your Uncle John says Esq. Blake would be the best and most influential man he knows of to call on. He is now away to Walpole. When he returns I will see him about it.

Willie, I am afraid to send you money for fear you will commit a rash act. Let me tell you, if you should attempt to desert & should not succeed to get off far, they would shoot you down. Perhaps if they did not, they would put you in irons. Then all would be lost for how long could you live in irons & in a cold damp cell? Try & keep up a good heart a little longer. It is an old saying & very true one I think that it is always darkest just before day. It may prove true in your case.

I was calculating to send you a box of things in a few days. But now I shant until I hear from you again. I told you I had 20 dollars left, I sent you 3 and let Marlon[1] have 2 which leaves 15 dollars. If I send that to you it will take all I have. So if you alter your mind & want me to send the box you will have to send back money for I do not think we can get it started without paying. You say you will soon be paid off again so you will have enough to come home if you should have a chance. But I charge you over & over again to not make the attempt unless you are sure of success. Weigh the matter well. Consider it would be a chance of life or death with you. If you get away go directly to your Uncle Downing's & keep as secluded as possible. And have them let me know you are there at once. And I will find out whether or not I could get you discharged through a process of Habeas Corpus. If you don't get away, don't you spend this money. Don't let anyone know you have got it.

I suppose you pity those sick soldiers and want to help them, but remember you yourself are in a bad place & will want it. Charity begins at home & you know I have no way to raise money for you. Tell me if your Capt. is what you thought he would be or does he look down upon his men as most of the officers do. What does Warren & Augustus say about staying or coming away? Are they pleasant or grouchy? What does Moore think of it? Don't you camp with Raymond boys? When Charlie Perkins came home from Concord he stopped one night & two days with the soldiers at Manchester. He saw enough of a soldier's life to satisfy him. Said they did not have half enough to eat and one night had no supper at all.

---

[1] Marlon—Willie's brother.

What kind of weather have you? Do you have any snow? Tie something over your ears and around your neck nights & you won't be so likely to get cold. You ought to stir up your straw & air your tents in the daytime as much as you can. If you & Gus try to get off together you will get caught. Is Warren low spirited or not? I shall tremble for your safety now every moment until I hear from you again. Willie, remember what I tell you about this money. I thought I should have it to help send someone to try to get you discharged. If you don't get off & spend your money you see you will be a great deal worse off. I feel bad to send it in two respects. For fear it will cause you to take a fatal step, if not you will spend it foolishly. I charge you again to calm your feelings. Be cool & collected as possible. I know it must be a strange sight to you to see so many sick, dead & dying persons but be not afraid, when the spirit is gone they are nothing but clay, the same that you & I shall be & every one else sometime. You know Willie all must die, although life is sweet & it is hard for friends to part. I hope it will be God's will that we shall meet again. You must trust in Him, he is the God of War & the people's God. I feel as though I could sacrifice every dollar I have if I could bring you safely home. I hope & trust you may be released, yet be patient, courageous, & hopeful. Your Uncle John advised me not to send the money. I suppose he thought you would not succeed & be worse off, or spend it. I want you to disappoint him.

Goodbye,
Mother

Camp of Instruction
Jan. 8, 1862

Dear Mother,

I received your kind letter today. I was very glad to hear from my mother and brother. You wanted to know how it was that I enjoyed good health in your letter and had a bad cold in Uncle John's. Well, I will tell you. I did not feel sick but I did not know but what if I got some medicine it would do my cold some good, so I went to the doctor and he gave me some chalk and water. I should think, by the taste at any rate, it done me no good but I guess I will be better in a day or two. Rest assured that when I am sick you shall know it.

You speak about my being discharged, that if I was discharged to come directly home. What did you mean by it? Did you think I would marry some [colored] gal and settle down out here? You need not worry, if I should be discharged I shall come home, if I can get home.

You seem to be thinking that when I come home I shall be a drunkard. You need not worry for I shall not drink at <u>all</u>. There is only two places in this camp where liquor can be bought and privates have to get an order from their Capt. before they will let it go if I need any for a medical purpose. You said you felt sometimes' as if you should fly away. If you should fly, just come out here and see me.

You wanted to know how I liked my Capt. I like him first-rate. He uses his men like a gentleman. The First Lt. is a nice man and works for the interest of his men. We drill four hours in a day.

I will now give you a description of Washington[2] as near as I can. I have not been on but two or three streets. The street that directs us to our camp is West 7th St.

[2] Willie's outfit was sent to Washington for training.

It reaches two or three miles and is nearly straight and level. The most popular street is Pennsylvania Avenue. It is about such a street as Broadway N.Y. As soon as a soldier gets on this street and has no pass from his Capt. he had better look out for the city guard for if they catch a man without a pass they take him as a deserter. A few days after I arrived here I went to the Capitol but could not see much for I did not have much time. I saw a large room full of pictures of the surrender of Lord Corn Wallace[3] and other war like pictures. And I stopped to look at them until my time was up. I shall get a pass and go over again in a few days.

I was over to the city yesterday and went into the Patent Office. I saw any quantity of things there. I saw the pants, vest and coat that Washington wore. Saw a lot of silks that the Japanese ambassadors gave to President Buchanan. Saw models of ships, plows, harrows, engines, steamboats and everything else you could think of that was patented except a soldier and they cannot be improved very well. They had the armor that soldiers used but did not have the soldier. I reviewed them as long as I thought proper and then went down on the street a little while and then came back to camp.

I have not got a look at the rail splitter[4] yet. I suppose he has enough to do to tend to affairs of his country without going out around to show himself. Neither have I seen the Secretary of War so I can't tell whether he would discharge that fellow you spoke about or not.

You wanted to know if the soldiers stole. I guess they won't steal from each other but they steal boards and wood. I like the country first-rate. Think I should like to live here if I could have a good house to sleep in. Warren has come back into the ranks again. He did not

---

[3] Lord Corn Wallace—Charles Cornwallis (1738–1805), a British general in the American Revolutionary War.

[4] the "rail splitter"—Abraham Lincoln.

like it in the hospital. No one is sick that you ever heard of except Hazen Currier. He is coming here. I have not been to see the Fifth Regiment yet. I should like to first-rate but it is ten miles over there.

About that box, you had better send it as soon as possible for there is no knowing when we shall be discharged and I need the things. Send by Adams Express for that is the most sure. When you leave the box get a receipt for it. I have answered Maria's letter. I received a letter from Clara Downing the same time I received yours. She said Uncle John was there then. She seemed to be a little surprised to find that I am at Washington. She said she could not imagine who it was from until she opened it and found my name. I cannot write all she said so I will send the letter. I like to get such a letter as you sent me as it is some fun to read such a letter. I can't find enough to write about to make such a letter.

Are the folks all well at Deerfield? How is grandfather's lip? How does grandmother get along through the cold weather? Tell Aunt Emma that that work bag comes in handy out here. Write as soon as you receive this. You write so I shall get a letter twice a week and I will do the same.

Yours in love
Wm. B Greene

Co. G 2d Regiment
Berdan's Brigade of U.S.S.S.
Camp of Instruction
Washington D.C.

Berdan[5] This our little Piggie.

---

[5] Hiram Berdan was criticized by many under his command for military incompetence and unbridled ambition. Says the editor of Greene's letters, "he was little different from many political officers who used the war for personal advancement and relied on others to do the real work."

Headquarters of Berdan's Humbug of United States
Sharp Shooters
Washington, D.C.
Jan. 11th 1862

Dear Mother,

I received your kind letter with $15 enclosed last night. You have no doubt received a letter from me before this stating that I did not want you to send me the money and that I should send it back if I received it. I will tell you how I came to send for it. Just as soon as I hear of any new diseases or of a large number of men dying at a time, I have to send right home and tell you all about it and by the time the letter is over to the city the briskness of the camp carries off my sad feelings and then I am sorry I wrote you. I am well now. My cold is better and I weigh 135 lbs. I have gained three or four lbs. since I left home. I was weighed the other day over at the Patent Office.

There is 32 sick in our company today. Warren True is sick this morning but I guess he will be better in a day or two. Don't you tell his folks for he would blame me for telling you. Gus is hearty as a pig. I am a great deal more hearty than when at home. If you wanted me to have my miniature[6] taken tell me and I will go over and get it taken. I have been on guard ever since I have been here. I have got to go on tomorrow morning. We have to stand on guard two hours on and four hours off. It's kind of funny that you have to show Uncle John every letter I write to you.

If I should take it into my head to come home and I had money enough I should come, but as long as there is any prospect of getting any guns I shant come home for I like this life first-rate. All that ails me is I can't stand it to see so many die. The boys are getting pretty unruly.

---

[6] miniature—photograph.

They don't care what they do as long as there is any chance to bring old Berdan into trouble. The other night they hung and then burnt Berdan in effigy and the day before yesterday a Capt. in the 1st Regiment led the whole regiment outside the guard and they pitched into the fence and took it all down as much as they could and brought it into camp [to use as firewood]. The man that owned it made a fuss and complained to Berdan. I don't know how they came out in it.

I shall not spend this money for I sewed it up in my drawers[7] where no one could get it. I shall stay here some time longer yet. I don't know when I shall get paid off but I will keep this money until I do. If I am sick I shall have something to help myself with. I have no more time for I have got to go on drill so goodbye until the next. You need not send the box until you hear from me again and when you do send it, put in a pie or two, for Aunt Samsuel[8] won't make them for us. She says she don't keep her boys on pie.

WBG

Sat. Eve Jan. 11

Dear Mother,

It is evening now so I will write a few more lines. I feel just like going to a promenade tonight. I have not drilled but ½ a day this week and that was today. We don't drill only ½ a day and Saturday at no time.

Augustus received a letter from Mary today. She wrote that you was troubled about me. What did she mean? If you are worrying about my deserting you need not for I shall not do it for the present. I will write to you before I do. If I could get transferred into the

---

[7] drawers—underpants.

[8] Aunt Samsuel—Uncle Sam.

N.H. 5th. I should be contented for I should not have to stay in one place so long. I know how Tilton feels for he is homesick. Some of our boys have been over there since we came here and they say that if they could get a chance to change with them they would do it. I signed a petition to send into Congress the other day to have them provide us with a better hospital and if they do we shall be all right. Send me some [news]papers, I have not had but only the two you sent me since I got here. My paper is all taken up so I must close. Write as soon as you receive this. I shall write to you again in a few days. Rest assured that if I am sick that I will tell you of it. How does True's folks feel about their boys getting humbugged[9] so?

Willie B. Greene

Camp at Bristol [Bristoe Station], VA
April 12th, 1862

Dear Mother,
I received your kind letter of April 7th yesterday and I now seat myself to answer it. You have, I trust, received my last letter wrote the day I arrived here on this camp ground. I wrote you as soon as we came to a halt after a hard march of about 50 miles. We have had a hard time. For two days and a half it has rained and blowed hard and the mud is some less than three feet deep. But it has cleared off and is pleasant. I guess we shall have it warm here now. I hope so at any rate.

We are living first-rate on sesech's[10] stuff. There has been plenty of sheep, pigs, turkeys, chickens, cattle and all such left here by those that have been compelled to

---

[9] humbugged—tricked.

[10] sesech's—Confederates' (short for secessioners').

go and leave here by the Union Army. But now there has been so many soldiers after them that they have either been killed or have gone out of their reach.

I tell you it is fun to go out and try our rifles. You have no doubt heard with what good success the First Regt. S.S. have met with in the last engagement at Yorktown and we will have as good, if not a better name than they, for when we were at Washington they said the 2nd Regt. was the best. We have just received the glorious news of the battle at Fittsburg [Pittsburgh Landing]. If the report we have is true, the rebels are destitute of Generals. Gen. Johnson killed. Gen. Beaureguard a prisoner and wounded. It seems to be a rather hard fate for them but it is well for the government from which they have left.

There are no white men here but there are a few women. We went to a house about two miles from camp and there was a woman and little boy there. Some of the boys asked her where her husband was and she said she had none. They said a widow then? No, said she, I never had one. Then, by G–d, you have got caught some time. Well, said she, I suppose I have. I tell you this so to let you see how the women work to hide the fact that their husbands are in the rebel army. . . .

Camp on the Battle Field
at Cedar Mountain Virginia
August 17, 1862

Dear Mother,
I now sit down to write you a few lines. We have moved since my last and we are now in camp on the field of the late engagement of Aug. 9th, or where it first commenced in a nice little peach orchard. When we first came in here the trees were loaded with peaches but they were not ripe. But they are most gone now for the boys have made sauce of them. But enough of this, I will

give you a slight explanation of what I have seen of the battle field.

I can now step outside my tent and look up on to the mountain and see right where the enemy had a battery stationed. The one that killed so many. The ground for two miles around here is covered with graves of soldiers killed and the carcasses of dead horses and, I tell you, if you want a good wholesome stink just go about ½ mile above here and there you will get it, for horses are very thick there where the cavalry made a dash and a shell flew in amongst them. There is not much to be seen, only horses and graves, excepting old cartridge boxes, haversacks, canteens, etc.

There is a union man lives close here and the rebels shelled his house and put three holes through the top and two through the side. He now has some wounded union soldiers at his house under his care.

I visited, day before yesterday, a southern grave yard where the enemy's soldiers were buried and I tell you, it looked nice. There was about 600 graves and all of them died of the effects of the Bull Run Battle. There was two union men there, it said on their head boards— Union Prisoners, died July 28, 1861 and July 25, 1861. They were taken at Bull Run and died here. The headboard and graves were fixed just the same as their own men. The yard was fenced in, but some miserable sinner had tore the fence down to build a tent, or for some other purpose.

We are now in a good place with good water here in the mountains and I tell you, if they are not cold nights here—and the days are pretty cold . . . but the nights. I have a shelter tent and a good pile of straw on the bottom. Then I spread down two rubbers and then we put two heavy blankets over us and we lay warm. But the boys in the Co., some of them lay cold. Some of them threw their woolen blankets away before coming here. Gus among the rest, and now they see the need of them.

Warren is sick and has been so for some time. He could not carry his load last march. Now, I don't want you to go right and tell his folks of it for he will be well soon probably and he will blame me for telling you.

I suppose Web and the rest of the 5th Band are home now for the bands were all disbanded day before yesterday. All went from here yesterday.

It is now after taps so I guess I will close. Good night.

From
Will

QUESTIONS TO CONSIDER

1. What do you think bothers Willie the most about life in the army?

2. What changes, if any, do you see in Willie from his first letter, dated January 3, 1862, to his letter of August 17, 1862?

3. What is Mrs. Greene's attitude toward Willie? Support your answer.

Diary of Wartime

BY CORNELIA PEAKE McDONALD

Cornelia McDonald began keeping a diary the night her husband, a lawyer, rode off with the Stonewall Brigade. He had asked her to keep the diary because he expected that "the town would be immediately occupied by the enemy," and he "wished to be informed of each day's events." As it turned out, her husband's prediction was correct. McDonald lived in Winchester, Virginia, with her seven children: Harry, thirteen; Allan, twelve; Kenneth, nine; Ellen, seven; Roy, five; Donald, two and a half; and Hunter, 21 months.

Winchester, March, 1862—On the night of March 11th, 1862, the pickets were in the town; part of the army had already gone, and there were hurried preparations and hasty farewells, and sorrowful faces turning away from those they loved best, and were leaving, perhaps forever. At one o'clock the long roll beat, and soon the heavy tramp of the marching columns died away in the distance.

The rest of the night was spent in violent fits of weeping at the thought of being left, and of what might happen to that army before we should see it again. I felt a terrible fear of the coming morning, for I knew that with it would come the much dreaded enemy.

I laid down when the night was almost gone, to sleep, after securing all the doors, and seeing that the children were all asleep. I took care to have my dressing gown convenient in case of an alarm, but the night passed away quietly, and when the morning came, and all was peaceful I felt reassured, dressed and went down.

The servants were up and breakfast was ready. The children assembled and we had prayers.

I felt so thankful that we were still free, and a hope dawned that our men would come back, as no enemy had appeared. We were all cheerfully despatching our breakfasts, I feeling happy in proportion to my former depression; the children were chatting gaily, Harry and Allan rather sulky at not having been permitted to leave with the army, as they considered it degradation for men of their years and dimensions to be left behind with women and children. Suddenly a strain of music! Every knife and fork was laid down and every ear strained to catch the faint sounds. The boys clap their hands and jump up from the table shouting, "Our men have come back!" and rushed to the door; I stopped them, telling them it must be the Yankees. Every face looked blank and disappointed.

I tried to be calm and quiet, but could not, and so got up and went outside the door. Sure enough that music could not be mistaken, it was the "Star Spangled Banner" that was played. A servant came in. "They are all marching through the town, and some have come over the hill into our orchard."

I made the children all sit down again, and began to eat my breakfast, but felt as if I should choke with anger and **mortification**.[1]

Tears of anger started from Harry's eyes, while Allan looked savage enough to exterminate them if he had the power. Kenneth looked very wretched, but glanced occasionally out of the window, as if he would like, as long as they had come, to see what they were like. Nelly's face was bent in the deepest humiliation on her plate, as if the shame of defeat was peculiarly hers. Roy's black eyes were blazing, as if he scented a fight but did not exactly know where to find it. While Donald, only two and a half years old, turned his back to weep silently, in sympathy I suppose with the distress of the rest. Presently a trampling was heard around the house, loud voices and the sounds of wheels and horses' hoofs. Suddenly a most unwonted sound! A mule braying; Nelly looked up from her plate where her eyes had been fixed in shame and distress: "Even their very old horses are laughing." That was irresistible. I was compelled in spite of all to join the horses in their laugh.

I was obliged to attend to my household affairs, and in passing to and fro on the porch and through passages, encountered them often, but took no notice, just moved on as if they were not there. Donald was sitting on a step very disconsolate looking, when one blue coat passed near him, and laying his hand on his head, said "How d'ye do Bub." He did not look up, but sullenly said, "Take your hand off my head, you are a Yankee." The man looked angry, but did not try to annoy us because the small rebel scorned him.

Ten o'clock had come, and we were still undisturbed. Only men passing through the yard to get water from the spring; so I put on my bonnet and went to town to see what had befallen my friends, and to attend to some necessary business. As I approached Mrs. Powell's

---

[1] **mortification**—shame or humiliation; wounded pride.

house, I saw a group of officers standing at the gate, brilliantly dressed men who, as I could not help seeing as I advanced, were regarding me very curiously. I was obliged to pass very near them, but did so without being, or seeming to be aware of their presence. When I had gone by, I heard behind me a "Whew" and a little quiet laugh. I knew they were laughing at my **loftiness,**[2] but tried to smother my resentment.

As I came near the town I encountered throngs of soldiers of different parts of the army. The pavements were lined with them, the doorsteps and front yards filled, and they looking as much at home, and as unconcerned as if the town and all in it belonged to them, and they were quietly enjoying their own.

Conspicuous above the rest were Banks'[3] bodyguard. A regiment of Zuaves,[4] with scarlet trousers, white leather gaiters,[5] and red fez.[6] I would not look at them, though I saw them distinctly.

As I passed Mrs. Seevers' beautiful house that was her pride and delight, I saw an unusual stir. More Zuaves were on the pavement in front, many stretched on the beautiful lawn or smelling the flowers that were just budding out. Two stood, straight and upright at each side of the door, while sentinels walked back and forth outside the gate. That I afterwards heard was Banks' headquarters.

I passed some friends who looked at me with unspoken mortification and distress. All houses were shut, and blinds down.

Occasionally at a door might be seen an excited woman talking resentfully to one, or a group of men. I

---

[2] **loftiness**—arrogance; haughtiness.

[3] Banks'—refers to N.P. Banks (1816–1894), an abolitionist and a Union general.

[4] Zuaves—a unit of the Union Army that dressed colorfully and marched in precise routines.

[5] gaiters—coverings for the leg extending from the instep to the ankle or knee.

[6] fez—a man's felt cap.

hated the sight of the old town, as it looked with strangers meeting me at every step, their eyes looking no friendliness; only curiosity or insolence. I finished my business, and without exchanging a word with any one, set out for home.

As I turned in at the gate at the end of the avenue, I beheld a sight that made my heart stand still. A number of horses were tied on the lawn, and in the porch was a group of men. I went straight up to the house, as I came near saw they were U. S. officers. There they stood in all the glory of their gold lace and epaulettes,[7] but I felt neither awed by their **martial**[8] appearance, or fascinated by their bravery of apparel. I walked deliberately up the steps until I reached the top one, as I felt that I could be less at a disadvantage in an encounter if on a level with them. When there I stood still and waited for them to speak. One took off his cap and came towards me coloring violently. "Is this Mrs. McDonald," said he. I bowed stiffly, still looking at him.

He handed me a card, "De Forest, U. S. Army." I bowed again and asked if he had any business with me, knowing well that he had, and guessing what it was. Another then came forward as if to relieve him, and said that they had been sent by General Williams to look at the house, with a view to occupying it as headquarters, and asked if I had any objection to permitting them to see the rooms. I told him that I had no objection to them seeing the rooms, but that I had very many objections to having it occupied as headquarters. (This was said very loftily.) But that as I could not prevent it, they must, if they chose do it. This was meant to be indignant, but at the end, angry tears would come. One or two seemed sorry for me, but the others looked little moved. I went and opened a room for their inspection, but they declined

---

[7] epaulettes—ornamental fringed shoulder pads worn as part of a military uniform.

[8] **martial**—war-like.

looking in, and asked what family I had, and how many rooms the house contained. I told them there were seven children, and that the two youngest were ill.

They bowed themselves out but Maj. Wilkins, the one who was the second to speak, turned back and coming close to me said, "I will speak to Gen. Williams and see if they cannot be accommodated elsewhere." Then they all left, but in a few hours a note came from Maj. Wilkins, saying that in consideration of sickness in my family, Gen. Williams would not inconvenience me. I was very grateful at being left to myself, but not glad to be obliged to feel grateful to these intruders.

For a week or more I was annoyed but little, though every day would hear tales of the arrest of citizens, and occupation of houses belonging to them, while their families were obliged to seek quarters elsewhere, so of course there was nothing like quietness or peace of mind. These outrages roused all our indignant feelings, but when we had a closer acquaintance with war, we wondered how such things could have disturbed us so much.

One morning, very early I observed a U. S. flag streaming over Mr. Mason's house. Found out that it was occupied as headquarters by a Massachusetts regiment. . . .

March, 1862—The Baltimore American, the only paper we see, is full of the amazing success of the "National Army" over the rebels. "The traitor Jackson[9] is fleeing up the valley with Banks in hot pursuit. The arch rebel suffers not the grass to grow under his flying feet. There is perfect confidence in his speedy downfall."

Gen. Shields is in command; Banks has gone—with nearly two-thirds of the army. Those that are here make a great display of their finery, and the grandeur of their

---

[9] Thomas Jonathan "Stonewall" Jackson (1824–1863) was a Confederate general, held second only to Robert E. Lee in the affection and esteem of Southerners.

equipments, but the people take no notice of them. I meet the gorgeous officers every day in our hall, but I never raise my eyes.

As I came up the avenue a few days since, I noticed one of the beautiful ornamental trees cut down for fuel. I was greatly disturbed by it; and as I entered the hall, still angry and excited, I met rather a fine looking officer coming out. He was a large man, handsomely dressed, and seemed inclined to be courteous. He raised his cap, and held the door open for me to pass, but remained standing after I had entered. I took the opportunity to speak of the trees and asked that no more be allowed to be destroyed. He said he would do his best to prevent it and as he still stood and wished to say something else, I waited to hear what it was. First he said he was astonished to see so much bitterness manifested toward them by the people, especially by the ladies of Winchester. "I do not think," he said, "that since I have been here I have seen a pleasant countenance. I always notice that the ladies on the street invariably turn away their faces when I look at them, or if they show them at all, have on all their sour looks. Do they always look sour and do they always dress so gloomily in black?" "As for the dress," said I, "many of them are wearing black for friends killed in battle, and others are not inclined to make a display of dress when those they love are in hourly danger; and they cannot look glad to see those they would like to have drowned in the sea, or overwhelmed with any calamity that would take them from our country." He said no more but passed on.

One day Maj. Wilkins called to bring me a written protection for the house and ground, consigning to death any who should violate it. Gen. Shields had given it. He also offered to take for me any letters to friends in the Stonewall Brigade, as he was to set out that day for the upper valley, and could communicate by flag of truce. I soon wrote one or two while he waited, putting nothing in them but that we were well, and in quiet, but anxious for intelligence of their well-being.

He sealed them in my presence, and when I asked him if it would not occasion him trouble he only laughed and said carelessly that it might cost him his commission, but that he would see that it did not.

I expressed great concern lest it should be a cause of trouble to him, and felt so grateful for his kindness, that I told him if he was ever sick or otherwise in need of a kind office to apply to me; he thanked me, and mounting his horse, galloped off to join Banks in his advance up the valley.

QUESTIONS TO CONSIDER

1. Do you feel sympathy for Cornelia McDonald? Why or why not?

2. At one point, Cornelia expresses anger that she should feel beholden to the officers. Later, she changes her attitude. What brings about that change?

3. What do you suppose Cornelia is alluding to when she admits, ". . . when we had a closer acquaintance with war, we wondered how such things could have disturbed us so much"?

Fighting the War

War Broke Out Fort Sumter, S.C., April 4, 1861, under the Confederate flag.

▲
Blue A Union volunteer of 1861.

Lieutenant General Ulysses S. Grant, in June, 1864, before he became chief commander of the Union forces. ▶

▲

General Robert E. Lee, commander of the Confederate forces.

Gray Private Charles Comes, Company K, 8th Louisiana Infantry, who was killed at Gettysburg, on July 1, 1863. ▶

Recruiting A billboard calls for volunteers in New York City. ▶

River Crossing Troops and guns cross the river on a raft.
▼

Regimental Drill The 96th Pennsylvania Infantry Regiment during drill at Camp Northumberland, 1861.

Recruiting Poster This Federal recruiting poster was issued at New Berne, N.C., in November 1863.

Naval Battle Ironclad warships were a new technology of war. History's first battle between them was fought March 9, 1862, when the Confederate ship *Virginia* (better known as the *Merrimack*) was met by the Federal ship *Monitor*. Supporters on both sides watched and cheered from the shores. The *Monitor* was disabled, but not vanquished. The *Virginia* won the first battle, and Confederate hopes soared.

Technology The Civil War saw the first submarines and aircraft carriers. Torpedo boats and advanced guns and shells also gave new tools for war.

The Battle of Antietam, September 17, 1862 (also called the Battle of Sharpsburg) Federal General George McClellan stopped Confederate General Robert E. Lee's advance on Maryland at Antietam. It was a dreadful battle with over 12,000 casualties on each side. McClellan allowed Lee to retreat and regroup, and for this he was later removed from his command by President Lincoln.

Antietam Bridge Soldiers and wagons cross the southern-most bridge over Antietam Creek.

Thousands Dead Confederate soldiers lay awaiting burial by a fence on the Hagerstown Road.

Lincoln Visits the Battlefield With the President are General McClellan and 15 of his staff. Just after the battle, on October 3, 1862, Lincoln issued the Emancipation Proclamation, ordering the Confederate states to return to the Union or their slaves would become free. The Proclamation took force in January, 1863.

▼

◀ Clara Barton

Field Hospital A surgeon performs an operation in a hospital tent at Gettysburg, July 1863.

▼

Caring for
the Wounded

BY CLARA BARTON

*Clara Barton dedicated most of her life to caring for those suffering—
first in battles, and later in peacetime disasters. While she is probably
best known for establishing the American Red Cross Society, her
work with wounded soldiers began when she was a volunteer during
the Civil War. Here is Barton's personal account of the Battle of
Chantilly, which followed closely on the second Battle of Bull Run.
Barton is among the Union troops.*

About three o'clock in the morning I observed a
surgeon with his little flickering candle in hand
approaching me with cautious step far up in the wood.
"Lady," he said as he drew near, "will you go with me?
Out on the hills is a poor distressed lad, mortally
wounded and dying. His piteous cries for his sister have
touched all our hearts, and none of us can relieve him,
but rather seem to distress him by our presence."

By this time I was following him back over the bloody track, with great beseeching eyes of anguish on every side looking up into our faces saying so plainly, "Don't step on us."

"He can't last half an hour longer," said the surgeon as we toiled on. "He is already quite cold, shot through the abdomen, a terrible wound." By this time the cries became plainly audible to me.

"Mary, Mary, sister Mary, come—oh, come, I am wounded, Mary! I am shot. I am dying—oh, come to me—I have called you so long and my strength is almost gone—Don't let me die here alone. Oh, Mary, Mary, come!"

Of all the tones of **entreaty**[1] to which I have listened—and certainly I have had some experience of sorrow—I think these, sounding through that dismal night, the most heart-rending. As we drew near, some 20 persons, attracted by his cries, had gathered around and stood with moistened eyes and helpless hands waiting the change which would relieve them all. And in the midst, stretched upon the ground, lay, scarcely full grown, a young man with a graceful head of hair, tangled and matted, thrown back from a forehead and a face of livid whiteness. His throat was bare. His hands, bloody, clasped his breast, his large, bewildered eyes turning anxiously in every direction. And ever from between his **ashen**[2] lips pealed that piteous cry of "Mary! Mary! Come."

I approached him unobserved, and, motioning the lights away, I knelt by him alone in the darkness. Shall I confess that I intended if possible to cheat him out of his terrible death agony? But my lips were truer than my heart, and would not speak the word "Brother" I had willed them to do. So I placed my hands upon his neck, kissed his cold forehead, and laid my cheek against his.

---

[1] **entreaty**—urgent pleading.

[2] **ashen**—very pale.

The illusion was complete; the act had done the falsehood my lips refused to speak. I can never forget that cry of joy. "Oh, Mary! Mary! You have come? I knew you would come if I called you and I have called you so long. I could not die without you, Mary. Don't cry, darling, I am not afraid to die now that you have come to me. Oh, bless you. Bless you, Mary." And he ran his cold, blood-wet hands about my neck, passed them over my face, and twined them in my hair, which by this time had freed itself from fastenings and was hanging damp and heavy upon my shoulders.

He gathered the loose locks in his stiffened fingers and holding them to his lips continued to whisper through them, "Bless you, bless you, Mary!" And I felt the hot tears of joy trickling from the eyes I had thought stony in death. This encouraged me, and, wrapping his feet closely in blankets and giving him such stimulants as he could take, I seated myself on the ground and lifted him on my lap, and drawing the shawl on my own shoulders also about his I bade him rest.

I listened till his blessings grew fainter, and in 10 minutes with them on his lips he fell asleep. So the gray morning found us; my precious charge had grown warm, and was comfortable.

Of course the morning light would reveal his mistake. But he had grown calm and was refreshed and able to endure it, and when finally he woke, he seemed puzzled for a moment, but then he smiled and said: "I knew before I opened my eyes that this couldn't be Mary. I know now that she couldn't get here, but it is almost as good. You've made me so happy. Who is it?"

I said it was simply a lady who, hearing that he was wounded, had come to care for him. He wanted the name, and with childlike simplicity he spelled it letter by letter to know if he were right. "In my pocket," he said, "you will find mother's last letter; please get it and write your name upon it, for I want both names by me when I die."

"Will they take away the wounded?" he asked. "Yes," I replied, "the first train for Washington is nearly ready now." "I must go," he said quickly. "Are you able?" I asked. "I must go if I die on the way. I'll tell you why; I am poor mother's only son, and when she consented that I go to the war, I promised her faithfully that if I were not killed outright, but wounded, I would try every means in my power to be taken home to her dead or alive. If I die on the train, they will not throw me off, and if I were buried in Washington, she can get me. But out here in the Virginia woods in the hands of the enemy, never. I must go!"

I sent for the surgeon in charge of the train and requested that my boy be taken. "Oh, impossible, madam, he is mortally wounded and will never reach the hospital! We must take those who have a hope of life." "But you must take him." "I cannot"—"Can you, Doctor, guarantee the lives of all you have on that train?" "I wish I could," said he sadly. "They are the worst cases; nearly 50 per cent must die eventually of their wounds and hardships."

"Then give this lad a chance with them. He can only die, and he has given good and sufficient reasons why he must go—and a woman's word for it, Doctor. You take him. Send your men for him." Whether yielding to argument or entreaty, I neither knew nor cared so long as he did yield nobly and kindly. And they gathered up the fragments of the poor, torn boy and laid him carefully on a blanket on the crowded train and with stimulants and food and a kind-hearted attendant, pledged to take him alive or dead to Armory Square Hospital and tell them he was Hugh Johnson, of New York, and to mark his grave. . . .

This finds us shortly after daylight Monday morning. Train after train of cars was rushing on for the wounded, and hundreds of wagons were bringing them in from the field still held by the enemy, where some poor sufferers had lain three days with no visible means of sustenance.[3] If immediately placed upon the trains and not detained, at least 24 hours must elapse before they could be in the hospital and properly nourished. They were already famishing, weak and sinking from loss of blood, and they could ill afford a further fast of 24 hours.

. . . I sought the various officers on the grounds, explained the case to them, and asked permission to feed all the men as they arrived before they should be taken from the wagons. It was well for the poor sufferers of that field that it was controlled by noble-hearted, generous officers, quick to feel and prompt to act.

They at once saw the propriety of my request and gave orders that all wagons should be stayed at a certain point and only moved on when every one had been seen and fed. This point secured, I commenced my day's work of climbing from the wheel to the brake of every wagon and speaking to and feeding with my own hands each soldier until he expressed himself satisfied.

Still there were bright spots along the darkened lines. Early in the morning the Provost Marshal came to ask me if I could use 50 men. He had that number, who for some slight breach of military discipline were under guard and useless, unless I could use them. I only regretted there were not 500. They came—strong, willing men—and these, added to our original force and what we had gained incidentally, made our number something over 80, and, believe me, 80 men and three women, acting with well-directed purpose, will accomplish a good deal in a day.

Our 50 prisoners dug graves and gathered and buried the dead, bore mangled men over the rough ground in their arms, loaded cars, built fires, made soup, and administered it. And I failed to discern that their services were less valuable than those of the other men. I had long suspected, and have been since convinced, that

---

[3] **sustenance**—food; provisions.

a private soldier may be placed under guard, court-martialed, and even be imprisoned without forfeiting his honor or manliness; that the real dishonor is often upon the gold lace rather than the army blue.[4]

At three o'clock the last train of wounded left. All day we had known that the enemy hung upon the hills and were waiting to break in upon us. . . . At four o'clock the clouds gathered black and murky, and the low growl of distant thunders was heard while lightning continually illuminated the horizon. The still air grew thick and stifled, and the very branches appeared to droop and bow as if in grief at the memory of the terrible scenes so lately enacted and the gallant lives so nobly yielded up beneath their shelter.

This was the afternoon of Monday. Since Saturday noon I had not thought of tasting food, and we had just drawn around a box for that purpose, when, of a sudden, air and earth and all about us shook with one mingled crash of God's and man's artillery. The lightning played and the thunder rolled incessantly and the cannon roared louder and nearer each minute. [The battle of] Chantilly with all its darkness and horrors had opened in the rear. . . .

The rain continued to pour in torrents, and the darkness became impenetrable save from the lightning leaping above our heads and the fitful flash of the guns, as volley after volley rang through the stifled air and lighted up the gnarled trunks and dripping branches among which we ever waited and listened.

In the midst of this, and how guided no man knows, came still another train of wounded men, and a waiting train of cars upon the track received them. This time nearly alone, for my worn-out assistants could work no longer, I continued to administer such food as I had left. . . . Army crackers put into knapsacks and haversacks

---

[4] gold lace . . . army blue—the officers rather than the enlisted men.

and beaten to crumbs between stones, and stirred into a mixture of wine, whiskey, and water, and sweetened with coarse brown sugar. Not very inviting you will think, but I assure you it was always acceptable. . . .

The departure of this train cleared the grounds of wounded for the night, and as the line of fire from its plunging engines died out in the darkness, a strange sensation of weakness and weariness fell upon me, almost defying my utmost exertion to move one foot before the other.

A little Sibley tent had been hastily pitched for me in a slight hollow upon the hillside. Your imaginations will not fail to picture its condition. Rivulets of water had rushed through it during the last three hours. Still I attempted to reach it, as its white surface, in the darkness, was a protection from the wheels of wagons and trampling of beasts.

Perhaps I shall never forget the painful effort which the making of those few rods and the gaining of the tent cost me. How many times I fell, from sheer exhaustion, in the darkness and mud of that slippery hillside, I have no knowledge, but at last I grasped the welcome canvas, and a well-established brook, which washed in on the upper side at the opening that served as door, met me on my entrance. My entire floor was covered with water, not an inch of dry, solid ground.

One of my lady assistants had previously taken the train for Washington and the other, worn out by faithful labors, was crouched upon the top of some boxes in one corner fast asleep. No such convenience remained for me, and I had no strength to arrange one. I sought the highest side of my tent which I remembered was grass-grown, and, ascertaining that the water was not very deep, I sank down. It was no laughing matter then. But the recollection of my position has since afforded me amusement.

I remember myself sitting on the ground, upheld by my left arm, my head resting on my hand, impelled by an almost uncontrollable desire to lie completely down, and prevented by the certain conviction that if I did, water would flow into my ears.

. . . I was aroused at 12 o'clock by the rumbling of more wagons of wounded men. I slept two hours, and oh, what strength I had gained! I may never know two other hours of equal worth. I sprang to my feet dripping wet, covered with ridges of dead grass and leaves, wrung the water from my hair and skirts, and went forth again to my work.

When I stood again under the sky, the rain had ceased, the clouds were sullenly retiring, and the lightning, as if deserted by its boisterous companions, had withdrawn to a distant corner and was playing quietly by itself. For the great volleying thunders of heaven and earth had settled down on the fields. Silent? I said so. And it was, save the ceaseless rumbling of the never-ending train of army wagons which brought alike the wounded, the dying, and the dead.

And thus the morning of the third day broke upon us, drenched, weary, hungry, sore-footed, sad-hearted, discouraged, and under orders to retreat.

A little later, the plaintive wail of a single fife, the slow beat of a muffled drum, the steady tramp, tramp, tramp of heavy feet, the gleam of 10,000 bayonets on the hills, and with bowed heads and speechless lips, poor Kearny's leaderless men came marching through.

This was the signal for retreat. All day they came, tired, hungry, ragged, defeated, retreating, they knew not whither—they cared not whither.

The enemy's cavalry, skirting the hills, admonished us each moment that we must soon decide to go from them or with them. But our work must be accomplished, and no wounded men once given into our hands must be left. And with the spirit of desperation, we struggled on.

At three o'clock an officer galloped up to me, with "Miss Barton, can you ride?" "Yes, sir," I replied.

"But you have no lady's saddle—could you ride mine?"

"Yes, sir, or without it, if you have blanket and surcingle."[5]

"Then you can risk another hour," he exclaimed, and galloped off.

At four he returned at a break-neck speed, and, leaping from his horse, said, "Now is your time. The enemy is already breaking over the hills; try the train. It will go through, unless they have flanked, and cut the bridge a mile above us. In that case I've a reserve horse for you, and you must take your chances to escape across the country."

In two minutes I was on the train. The last wounded man at the station was also on. The conductor stood with a torch which he applied to a pile of combustible material beside the track. And we rounded the curve which took us from view and we saw the station ablaze, and a troop of cavalry dashing down the hill. The bridge was uncut and midnight found us at Washington.

You have the full record of my sleep—from Friday night till Wednesday morning—two hours. You will not wonder that I slept during the next 24.

On Friday (the following), I repaired to Armory Square Hospital to learn who, of all the hundreds sent, had reached that point. I traced the chaplain's record, and there upon the last page freshly written stood the name of Hugh Johnson.

Turning to Chaplain Jackson, I asked, "Did that man live until today?" "He died during the latter part of last night," he replied. "His friends reached him some two days ago, and they are now taking his body from the ward to be conveyed to the depot."

---

[5] surcingle—a strap that binds a saddle, pack, or blanket to the body of a horse.

I looked in the direction his hand indicated, and there, beside a coffin, about to be lifted into a wagon, stood a gentleman, the mother, and sister Mary!

"Had he his reason?" I asked.

"Oh, perfectly."

"And his mother and sister were with him two days?"

"Yes."

There was no need of me. He had given his own messages; I could add nothing to their knowledge of him, and would **fain**[6] be spared the scene of thanks. Poor Hugh, thy piteous prayers reached and were answered, and with eyes and heart full, I turned away, and never saw sister Mary.

These were days of darkness—a darkness that might be felt. The shattered bands of Pope[7] and Banks! Burnside's[8] weary legions! Reinforcements from West Virginia—and all that now remained of the once glorious Army of the Peninsula had gathered for shelter beneath the redoubts and guns that girdled Washington.

---

[6] **fain**—gladly.

[7] Pope—John Pope (1822–1892) was a Union general. In 1862, as commander of the Army of Virginia, he suffered defeat at the Second Battle of Bull Run. He was relieved of his command shortly thereafter.

[8] Ambrose Everett Burnside (1824–1881) was a Union army officer. Under his command, the Federals sustained devastating losses at the First Battle of Bull Run (August 1861).

QUESTIONS TO CONSIDER

1. What do you think Barton believes is her greatest challenge in caring for the wounded?

2. What does Barton mean when she says, "... the real dishonor is often upon the gold lace rather than the army blue"?

3. In addition to first aid, what does Barton offer to the wounded soldiers?

from

The Red Badge
of Courage

BY STEPHEN CRANE

In one of the most famous novels about the Civil War, Stephen Crane presents his hero, Henry Fleming. He is the "youth" who wants to earn a wound—the "red badge of courage"—to prove his patriotism and manhood. With conflicting emotions of fear and duty, with desire for heroism and horror at what he sees, Henry is caught in what seems like a nightmare. Although Crane was born in 1871, after the war was over, and although he himself had never seen battle, he writes battle scenes so real and powerful that they seem to be based on personal experience.

There were moments of waiting. The youth thought of the village street at home before the arrival of the circus parade on a day in the spring. He remembered how he had stood, a small, thrillful boy, prepared to follow the dingy lady upon the white horse, or the band in its faded chariot. He saw the yellow road, the lines of expectant people, and the sober houses. He particularly remembered an old fellow who used to sit upon a cracker box in front of the store and feign to despise such exhibitions. A thousand details of color and form surged in his mind. The old fellow upon the cracker box appeared in middle prominence.

Some one cried, "Here they come!"

There was rustling and muttering among the men. They displayed a feverish desire to have every possible cartridge ready to their hands. The boxes were pulled around into various positions, and adjusted with great care. It was as if seven hundred new bonnets were being tried on.

The tall soldier, having prepared his rifle, produced a red handkerchief of some kind. He was engaged in knitting it about his throat with exquisite attention to its position, when the cry was repeated up and down the line in a muffled roar of sound.

"Here they come! Here they come!" Gun locks clicked.

Across the smoke-infested fields came a brown swarm of running men who were giving shrill yells. They came on, stooping and swinging their rifles at all angles. A flag, tilted forward, sped near the front.

As he caught sight of them the youth was momentarily startled by a thought that perhaps his gun was not loaded. He stood trying to rally his faltering intellect so that he might recollect the moment when he had loaded, but he could not.

A hatless general pulled his dripping horse to a stand near the colonel of the 304th. He shook his fist in the other's face. "You've got to hold 'em back!" he shouted, savagely; "you've got to hold 'em back!"

In his agitation the colonel began to stammer. "A-all r-right, General, all right, by Gawd! We-we'll do our—

we-we'll d-d-do–do our best, General." The general made a passionate gesture and galloped away. The colonel, perchance to relieve his feelings, began to scold like a wet parrot. The youth, turning swiftly to make sure that the rear was unmolested, saw the commander regarding his men in a highly resentful manner, as if he regretted above everything his association with them.

The man at the youth's elbow was mumbling, as if to himself. "Oh, we're in for it now! oh, we're in for it now!"

The captain of the company had been pacing excitedly to and fro in the rear. He coaxed in school-mistress fashion, as to a congregation of boys with primers. His talk was an endless repetition. "Reserve your fire, boys—don't shoot till I tell you—save your fire—wait till they get close up—don't be damned fools—"

Perspiration streamed down the youth's face, which was soiled like that of a weeping **urchin.**[1] He frequently, with a nervous movement, wiped his eyes with his coat sleeve. His mouth was still a little ways open.

He got the one glance at the foe-swarming field in front of him, and instantly ceased to debate the question of his piece being loaded. Before he was ready to begin—before he had announced to himself that he was about to fight—he threw the obedient, well-balanced rifle into position and fired a first wild shot. Directly he was working at his weapon like an automatic affair.

He suddenly lost concern for himself, and forgot to look at a menacing fate. He became not a man but a member. He felt that something of which he was a part—a regiment, an army, a cause, or a country—was in a crisis. He was welded into a common personality which was dominated by a single desire. For some moments he could not flee no more than a little finger can commit a revolution from a hand.

---

[1] **urchin**—mischievous youngster.

If he had thought the regiment was about to be anni-
hilated perhaps he could have amputated himself from
it. But its noise gave him assurance. The regiment was
like a firework that, once ignited, proceeds superior to
circumstances until its blazing vitality fades. It wheezed
and banged with a mighty power. He pictured the
ground before it as strewn with the **discomfited.**[2]

There was a consciousness always of the presence of
his comrades about him. He felt the subtle battle brother-
hood more potent even than the cause for which they
were fighting. It was a mysterious fraternity born of the
smoke and danger of death.

He was at a task. He was like a carpenter who has
made many boxes, making still another box, only there
was furious haste in his movements. He, in his thought,
was careering off in other places, even as the carpenter
who as he works whistles and thinks of his friend or his
enemy, his home or a saloon. And these jolted dreams
were never perfect to him afterward, but remained a
mass of blurred shapes.

Presently he began to feel the effects of the war
atmosphere—a blistering sweat, a sensation that his
eyeballs were about to crack like hot stones. A burning
roar filled his ears.

Following this came a red rage. He developed the
acute exasperation of a pestered animal, a well-meaning
cow worried by dogs. He had a mad feeling against his
rifle, which could only be used against one life at a time.
He wished to rush forward and strangle with his
fingers. He craved a power that would enable him to
make a world-sweeping gesture and brush all back. His
impotency appeared to him, and made his rage into that
of a driven beast.

Buried in the smoke of many rifles his anger was
directed not so much against the men whom he knew

---

[2] the **discomfited**—the people made uneasy or perplexed; the disconcerted.

were rushing toward him as against the swirling battle phantoms which were choking him, stuffing their smoke robes down his parched throat. He fought frantically for respite for his senses, for air, as a babe being smothered attacks the deadly blankets.

There was a blare of heated rage mingled with a certain expression of intentness on all faces. Many of the men were making low-toned noises with their mouths, and these subdued cheers, snarls, **imprecations,**[3] prayers, made a wild, barbaric song that went as an undercurrent of sound, strange and chantlike with the resounding chords of the war march. The man at the youth's elbow was babbling. In it there was something soft and tender like the monologue of a babe. The tall soldier was swearing in a loud voice. From his lips came a black procession of curious oaths. Of a sudden another broke out in a **querulous**[4] way like a man who has mislaid his hat. "Well, why don't they support us? Why don't they send supports? Do they think—"

The youth in his battle sleep heard this as one who dozes hears.

There was a singular absence of heroic poses. The men bending and surging in their haste and rage were in every impossible attitude. The steel ramrods clanked and clanged with incessant din as the men pounded them furiously into the hot rifle barrels. The flaps of the cartridge boxes were all unfastened, and bobbed idiotically with each movement. The rifles, once loaded, were jerked to the shoulder and fired without apparent aim into the smoke or at one of the blurred and shifting forms which upon the field before the regiment had been growing larger and larger like puppets under a magician's hand.

The officers, at their intervals, rearward, neglected to stand in picturesque attitudes. They were bobbing

---

[3] **imprecations**—curses.

[4] **querulous**—fretful, whining.

to and fro roaring directions and encouragements. The dimensions of their howls were extraordinary. They expended their lungs with **prodigal**[5] wills. And often they nearly stood upon their heads in their anxiety to observe the enemy on the other side of the tumbling smoke.

The lieutenant of the youth's company had encountered a soldier who had fled screaming at the first volley of his comrades. Behind the lines these two were acting a little isolated scene. The man was blubbering and staring with sheeplike eyes at the lieutenant, who had seized him by the collar and was pommeling him. He drove him back into the ranks with many blows.

The soldier went mechanically, dully, with his animal-like eyes upon the officer. Perhaps there was to him a divinity expressed in the voice of the other—stern, hard, with no reflection of fear in it. He tried to reload his gun, but his shaking hands prevented. The lieutenant was obliged to assist him.

The men dropped here and there like bundles. The captain of the youth's company had been killed in an early part of the action. His body lay stretched out in the position of a tired man resting, but upon his face there was an astonished and sorrowful look, as if he thought some friend had done him an ill turn. The babbling man was grazed by a shot that made the blood stream widely down his face. He clapped both hands to his head. "Oh!" he said, and ran. Another grunted suddenly as if he had been struck by a club in the stomach. He sat down and gazed ruefully. In his eyes there was mute, indefinite reproach. Farther up the line a man, standing behind a tree, had had his knee joint splintered by a ball. Immediately he had dropped his rifle and gripped the tree with both arms. And there he remained, clinging desperately and crying for assistance that he might withdraw his hold upon the tree.

---

[5] **prodigal**—extraordinary in quantity or degree.

At last an exultant yell went along the quivering line. The firing dwindled from an uproar to a last vindictive popping. As the smoke slowly eddied away, the youth saw that the charge had been **repulsed**.[6] The enemy were scattered into reluctant groups. He saw a man climb to the top of the fence, straddle the rail, and fire a parting shot. The waves had receded, leaving bits of dark débris upon the ground.

Some in the regiment began to whoop frenziedly. Many were silent. Apparently they were trying to contemplate themselves.

After the fever had left his veins, the youth thought that at last he was going to suffocate. He became aware of the foul atmosphere in which he had been struggling. He was grimy and dripping like a laborer in a foundry. He grasped his canteen and took a long swallow of the warmed water. A sentence with variations went up and down the line. "Well, we've helt 'em back. We've helt 'em back; derned if we haven't." The men said it blissfully, leering at each other with dirty smiles.

The youth turned to look behind him and off to the right and off to the left. He experienced the joy of a man who at last finds leisure in which to look about him.

Under foot there were a few ghastly forms motionless. They lay twisted in fantastic contortions. Arms were bent and heads were turned in incredible ways. It seemed that the dead men must have fallen from some great height to get into such positions. They looked to be dumped out upon the ground from the sky.

From a position in the rear of the grove a **battery**[7] was throwing shells over it. The flash of the guns startled the youth at first. He thought they were aimed directly at him. Through the trees he watched the black figures of the gunners as they worked swiftly and intently. Their labor

---

[6] **repulsed**—driven back.

[7] **battery**—an army artillery unit.

seemed a complicated thing. He wondered how they could remember its formula in the midst of confusion.

The guns squatted in a row like savage chiefs. They argued with abrupt violence. It was a grim pow-wow. Their busy servants ran hither and thither.

A small procession of wounded men were going drearily toward the rear. It was a flow of blood from the torn body of the brigade.

To the right and to the left were the dark lines of other troops. Far in front he thought he could see lighter masses protruding in points from the forest. They were suggestive of unnumbered thousands.

Once he saw a tiny battery go dashing along the line of the horizon. The tiny riders were beating the tiny horses.

From a sloping hill came the sound of cheerings and clashes. Smoke welled slowly through the leaves.

Batteries were speaking with thunderous oratorical effort. Here and there were flags, the red in the stripes dominating. They splashed bits of warm color upon the dark lines of troops.

The youth felt the old thrill at the sight of the emblem. They were like beautiful birds strangely undaunted in a storm.

As he listened to the din from the hillside, to a deep pulsating thunder that came from afar to the left, and to the lesser clamors which came from many directions, it occurred to him that they were fighting, too, over there, and over there, and over there. Heretofore he had supposed that all the battle was directly under his nose.

As he gazed around him the youth felt a flash of astonishment at the blue, pure sky and the sun gleamings on the trees and fields. It was surprising that Nature had gone tranquilly on with her golden process in the midst of so much devilment.

QUESTIONS TO CONSIDER

1. What caused Henry to become "not a man but a member"?

2. What are some of the things that surprise Henry about the battle?

3. Do you think Henry is proud or ashamed of his participation in the skirmish?

The Colored Troops

BY MILTON MELTZER

African Americans fought on both sides. Some went with their masters in the Confederate Army and performed support work that many soldiers in modern armies perform—tending camp, cooking meals, carrying supplies. Other slaves were given arms and fought along- side the regular soldiers. The Union Armies made room for "colored" troops about midway through the war. And finally, in the last days, the Confederate side did as well. Social historian Milton Meltzer uses source readings and first-person accounts to tell of the bravery and heroism of black soldiers in the Civil War.

From the sound of the first gun, Blacks had volun- teered to fight. But Northern sentiment said no, you can't; this is "a white man's war." Frederick Douglass asked, "What on earth was the matter with the American government and people? Do they really covet the world's ridicule as well as their own social and polit- ical ruin?" Ask the president, he said, "if this dark and terrible hour of the nation's extremity is a time for consulting a mere vulgar and unnatural prejudice. . . . This is no time to fight with one hand when both are needed. This is no time to fight with only your white hand, and allow your black hand to remain tied."

When given the chance, Blacks joined up eagerly. In the spring of 1862 a regiment of volunteers in South Carolina formed under the abolitionist General David Hunter, but after three months of service they were disbanded by government order. Another such group, formed by General Jim Lane in Kansas, suffered the same fate, though they saw action twice against Rebel guerrillas.

Finally, after the Emancipation Proclamation,[1] Union ranks were opened to Blacks. But promises of equal treatment were not kept. Black servicemen suffered unequal pay, allowances, and opportunities throughout the war. Theirs was a two-sided fight: against slavery in the South and against discrimination in the North.

That they fought hard and well was soon proved to a doubting nation. This was just as true of freed slaves in the South who joined up as it was of Northern Blacks. The 2nd Louisiana, made up of ex-slaves, took part in the siege of Port Hudson, a key point in the campaign for control of the Mississippi. On May 27, 1863, a broad assault was made upon the fortifications. General Nathaniel P. Banks, in a letter to General H. W. Halleck in Washington, evaluated the performance of his black troops:

> The artillery opened fire between 5 and 6 o'clock, which was continued with animation during the day. At 10 o'clock Weitzel's brigade, with two regiments of colored troops, made an assault upon the right of the enemy's works, crossing Sandy Creek, and driving them through the woods to their fortifications.

---

[1] Emancipation Proclamation—historic document that gave the Union forces the power to free slaves and admit freed slaves into the military.

The fight lasted on this line until 4 o'clock, and was very severely contested. The enemy was driven into his works, and our troops moved up to the fortifications. On the extreme right of our line I posted the first and third regiments of Negro troops. The First Regiment of Louisiana Engineers, composed exclusively of colored men, excepting the officers, was also engaged in the operations of the day. The position occupied by these troops was one of importance, and called for the utmost steadiness and bravery in those to whom it was confided.

It gives me pleasure to report that they answered every expectation. Their conduct was heroic. No troops could be more determined or more daring. They made, during the day, three charges upon the batteries of the enemy, suffering very heavy losses, and holding their position at nightfall with the other troops on the right of our line. The highest commendation is bestowed upon them by all the officers in command on the right. Whatever doubt may have existed before as to the efficiency of organizations of this character, the history of this day proves conclusively to those who were in a condition to observe the conduct of these regiments, that the Government will find in this class of troops effective supporters and defenders.

The severe test to which they were subjected, and the determined manner in which they encountered the enemy, leave upon my mind no doubt of their ultimate success.

Ten days later, at Milliken's Bend, a small Louisiana town farther up the river, a bloody hand-to-hand fight took place between Rebel and Union forces. It was one of the bitterest struggles during a war famous for hard-fought actions. Three incomplete black regiments of ex-slaves from Louisiana and Mississippi were sent into the battle only sixteen days after they were mustered in. And thirty-nine percent of them were killed or wounded. "The bravery of the Blacks at Milliken's Bend," said Assistant Secretary of War Charles A. Dana, "completely revolutionized the sentiment of the army with regard to the employment of Negro troops. "

Lincoln did not miss the lesson of Port Hudson and Milliken's Bend. He wrote out a message to be read at a public meeting in Springfield, Illinois:

> I know as fully as anyone can know the opinions of others, that some of the commanders of our armies in the field, who have given us our most important successes, believe that the emancipation policy and the use of colored troops constitute the heaviest blow yet dealt to the rebellion, and that at least one of these important successes could not have been achieved when it was but for the aid of black soldiers. . . .

By the war's end 180,000 Blacks had served in Lincoln's army and 30,000 in the navy, while 250,000 helped the military as laborers. To put an end to slavery, 38,000 Blacks gave their lives in battle. Twenty-one received the Congressional Medal of Honor. What they did helped to transform both the way the nation treated Blacks and the way Blacks saw themselves.

QUESTIONS TO CONSIDER

1. Reread the first paragraph. What is the cause of Frederick Douglass's outrage?

2. Why didn't the Union want black soldiers to fight in the war?

3. What does Meltzer mean when he says black servicemen had to fight a "two-sided fight"?

The Crater

BY J. TRACY POWER

At the time of the Civil War, land mines were a new weapon, and the troops who were attacked by one were "blown away" in more ways than one. This selection includes eyewitness accounts of the battle known as "the Crater" because it was fought in and around the huge hole in the ground produced by the explosion of a land mine. Not only was the weapon a new experience for Lee's soldiers, but this was also their first encounter with African-American troops. The time was June–July, 1864. The place was Petersburg, Virginia.

As the month of July came to an end, Lee's soldiers had several different predictions for their own immediate future. Some of them saw no indications that significant fighting would occur along the lines at Petersburg, such as the South Carolina sergeant who noted, "I do not know whither we will have any fighting imediatly[1] on this Line or not but it is the prevailing oppinion amongst the men that the enemy will not attact us here

---

[1] The author did not change the spelling and punctuation of the soldiers' letters he quoted.

for our Lines are to Strong for them to do so with any hope of Success." Others, such as the assistant adjutant general of a North Carolina brigade in the Third Corps, admitted that though they did not know what might happen, they did not trouble themselves about it. "Nothing seems to startle the imperturbable soldier," Capt. Louis G. Young commented to his mother on 29 July. "A great battle here tomorrow would not surprise me, while I would be signally unmoved by order to leave for Northern Va. & Maryland."

Young's "great battle" did indeed take place the next day. It was initiated by one of the most extraordinary incidents of the entire war, in which the Federals made an ingenious attempt to force the Confederates from their strong defensive position. A detachment of Grant's soldiers had spent almost a month digging a long tunnel to a point underneath the enemy salient,[2] where they planned to set off a mine and literally blast a hole in Lee's lines. An infantry division, specially trained for the task, would then assault what remained of the Confederates in the immediate vicinity and attempt to force its way through to the city itself.

Earlier, some observers in the Army of Northern Virginia, noticing an unusual amount of enemy activity at one particular point along the lines, had suspected that Grant might be digging a mine. Engineers were quickly authorized to dig countermines and listening galleries in an effort to prevent the Federals from completing their work. "We are tunnelling & Grant is also," Virginia artilleryman James Albright reported in his diary on 20 July, "& some mines may be sprung any day, & many souls blown into eternity." A few days later Albright commented, "we are not near enough in our mines to hear the enemies *picks*—still the *springing* of a mine, while it might startle us, would not surprise any one—at any moment."

---

[2] salient—an outwardly projecting part of a fortification or line of defense.

The Federals' mine, which did a great deal more than startle Lee's soldiers, was detonated at about 4:45 A.M. on 30 July. The fierce fight that followed, known forever after as "the Crater" from the massive hole carved out of the ground by the explosion of four tons of gunpowder, would in time become the best known of all the engagements around Petersburg. An infantry brigade and an artillery battery of Beauregard's command that occupied the salient were virtually destroyed, with most of the dead in those unfortunate units either killed by the blast or buried under a huge mass of earth. As soon as the smoke and dust had cleared somewhat, a Federal division advanced into the gap, which was later estimated to be about 125 feet long, about 50 feet wide, and about 25 feet deep. But the attackers milled around in the crater in confusion instead of bypassing it and were soon joined by reinforcements that repeated their mistake.

After the shocked defenders in the area regrouped and were reinforced by a division of the Third Corps, the Confederates secured their works, counterattacked with infantry and artillery that surrounded the crater, and inflicted appalling casualties on the Federals. Savage hand-to-hand fighting, reminiscent of the scene at Spotsylvania,[3] took place not across log breastworks but in and around a chasm full of debris, of the dead and wounded and of soldiers struggling desperately with each other, in what one participant described as "the dreadfulest seen I ever wittnest." Many of Lee's soldiers, infuriated by the sight of black Federals—the first they had met in combat—shot or bayoneted them as they tried to surrender or after they had already done so. Within a few hours, by early afternoon at the latest, the Confederates had recovered all of the ground lost to Grant's bold attack and forced those Federals who had not been killed or taken prisoner back to their own lines.

---

[3] Spotsylvania—a village in Virginia southwest of Fredericksburg that was the site of a major battle May 8–21, 1864.

Grant's casualties numbered some 3,800 killed, wounded, and captured out of an assaulting force of about 16,500 troops; Lee's defenders suffered about 1,500 casualties out of a defending force of about 9,500, with nearly half of that number being lost in the initial explosion by Stephen Elliott's South Carolina brigade and by Capt. Richard G. Pegram's company of Virginia artillery. What had promised to be a significant, perhaps decisive, Federal victory had instead become another frustrating battlefield defeat. By the same token, what had threatened to be a Confederate disaster developed instead into yet another tactical success that had almost no lasting effect on the conduct of the war.

This spectacular battle was, of course, the topic of widespread discussion throughout the Army of Northern Virginia for some time to come. Though remarkably few Confederate units were engaged at the Crater—only one entire division and several brigades of two others, along with various artillery battalions and batteries— there were other factors that contributed to the almost universal interest shown by correspondents and diarists. Among these factors were the sheer novelty of the mine and the chaos created by its explosion; the relative ease with which the Confederate counterattack broke the Federal assault, capturing hundreds of prisoners and nearly a score of enemy flags; and the behavior of black Federals and their white officers, as well as the reaction of Lee's soldiers to such behavior. Most observers in the army would have agreed with the comment of the brigadier who wrote his father a few days later, "Since I last wrote, we have had some excitement and some very heavy fighting."

Accounts of the Crater written by the few survivors in Elliott's Brigade and the other soldiers in Bushrod Johnson's Division, naturally enough, emphasized the surprise that accompanied the sudden explosion of the salient underneath them and the appearance of the

Federals in their lines. "Just at sunrise as I had steped up on the step of the breastwork I herd a tremendous dull report and at the same time felt the earth shake beneath me," a sergeant in the 26th Virginia, in Wise's Brigade, observed. "I immediately looked down to our left & to my sorrow I saw an awful scene, which I never witnessed before." Johnson's own official report, written a few weeks after the battle, described "The astonishing effect of the explosion, bursting like a volcano at the feet of the men, and the upheaving of an immense column of more than 100,000 cubic feet of earth to fall around in heavy masses, wounding, crushing, or burying everything within its reach." Johnson commended his troops for their conduct, claiming, "It is believed for each buried companion they have taken a twofold vengeance on the enemy, and have taught them a lesson that will be remembered as long as the history of our wrongs and this great revolution endures." One of those "buried companions" was 2d Sgt. John W. Callahan of the 22d South Carolina. Callahan's friend Daniel Boyd, himself a sergeant in Joseph Kershaw's old brigade of the First Corps, wrote that "J W Calahan Was Kild by the blowing up of our breast Works he was buried wit[h] the dirt. When they found him he was Standing Strait up the ditch their was one hundred kild and buried with the explosion." A captain in the 49th North Carolina, in Brig. Gen. Matt W Ransom's Brigade, observed, "When the dust and smoke cleared away several of the enemy's flags were floating on our line. They re-enforced rapidly and overwhelmed our men in the trenches on either side of the chasm." Though the blast and the Federal assault essentially wrecked Elliott's Brigade, the other brigades in Johnson's Division retained enough order to mount a stubborn defense until badly needed reinforcements arrived.

Those reinforcements, most notably three brigades of William Mahone's Division of the Third Corps, launched a vicious counterattack that was the focal point of the fighting at the Crater and that rightfully received the lion's share of attention after the battle. Numerous officers and men in these units, particularly Mahone's infantrymen, understandably believed that they had saved the Army of Northern Virginia on 30 July. "Alas many a noble Confederate sealed his devotion to his countries cause with his life in the struggle," commented Robert C. Mabry of the 6th Virginia. Two days later Mabry, who had been on picket duty at the time of the battle, wrote his wife, "it pains me to say that my company was almost entirely swept away; it carried in the Fight Twenty one muskets & three *commissd* officers, came out with two men & one officer. . . . I hear there are only Ten privates left in the entire Regt." A contemporary history of the 48th Georgia called the battle "certainly one of the most **sanguinary**[4] fights on record," claiming, "Nothing could withstand the desperate valor of our boys."

Lt. Elias Davis of the 10th Alabama remarked to his wife: "Last Saturday (30th of July) is a day that will be long remembered by members of our brigade. . . . Our Brigade is said to have made the grandest charge of the war, capturing three stands of colors & five hundred Yankees & negroes." Those captured Federal colors— nineteen flags or portions of flags in all, taken by David A. Weisiger's Virginia brigade, by John C. C. Sanders's Alabama brigade, and by A.R. Wright's Georgia brigade—were a particularly dramatic measure of the division's performance at the Crater. Secretary of War James Seddon endorsed a list of the flags and their captors with the comment, "let appropriate acknowledgement be made to the gallant general and his brave troops." A Virginia artillery officer in the Third Corps believed that the battle demonstrated "the superiority of

---

[4] **sanguinary**—bloody.

veterans to new troops—i.e. of Lee's to [General P. G. T.] Beauregard's troops. They had to take Mahone's Division from this portion of the line, to that point, near the centre, to retake & reestablish the line, because those troops failed."

Many Confederate observers, both those who fought at the Crater and nonparticipants, made frequent references in their letters and diaries to the brutal combat there and to the appalling sight of dead and wounded soldiers in the crater itself. "We witnessed the charge of the negroes—we saw the desperate hand to hand fight—saw the bayonets lock—the thrusts given—the rifles clubbed," Capt. Henry A. Chambers, a North Carolinian in Johnson's Division, recorded in his diary on 30 July. "Maddened by the sight our men were nerved to fight in desperation." The battle flag of the 48th Georgia was said to have been "pierced by one hundred and three bullets, and three times was the staff cut two in this engagement." Shocked correspondents and diarists described the bodies of the Federal dead as they lay "in piles blacks whites and all together lying in piles three and four deep," "literally crammed in our trenches and bomb proofs," or "piled indiscriminately together, one hundred and thirty-three were buried in the bottom of the chasm." One Georgia private thought that "the whole face of the Earth was utterly strewn with dead negroes Ys. [Yankees] and our men," and a fellow Georgian, a corporal in another brigade, claimed, "our men left them thicker than any place that ever yanks was killed on . . . in that hole there is three hundred yankees ded besids the wounded." A Virginia artillery officer spoke for many witnesses when he told his sister, "I never saw such a sight as I saw on that portion of the line."

QUESTIONS TO CONSIDER

1. What caused Grant's defeat at the Crater?

2. Why did this battle in particular capture so much interest and attention?

3. How did Lee's army react to the black Federal soldiers? Why do you think they reacted this way?

Andersonville

BY SOLON HYDE

In 1861, Solon Hyde enlisted as a hospital steward with the 17th Ohio Volunteer Infantry. He took part in the Battle of Chickamauga, where he was captured by General Nathan Bedford Forrest's cavalry. He spent the next seventeen months in Libby, Pemberton, Danville, and finally Andersonville prisons. The Confederate prison near Andersonville, Georgia, was notorious. Nearly 49,500 Union troops were imprisoned there between February 1864 and the end of the war. Of these, 13,709 died. As Hyde shows us, there was no protection from the natural elements; a stinking, foul channel of water ran through the camp carrying filth and disease, and scurvy and dysentery were rampant. Here is his description of his first days in camp.

We reached Andersonville about the 25th of July, 1864. This now historic place was simply a railroad station on the road from Macon to Americus, the settlement consisting merely of six or eight houses, mostly military necessities, and an unfinished church; the whole being surrounded by dense pine woods with a heavy growth of underbrush. The **stockade**[1] was located about half a mile east of the depot, in plain sight, looking down the stream that arose near the town and passed through the stockade after receiving another branch from the north side of the town.

. . . Our feelings, as we made the march to the north gate, cannot be imagined. As it swung open with a loud creaking noise that could be heard all over the camp, what a view of misery met our eyes! Great God! could it be possible that this motley, haggard crowd that pressed around us had once been soldiers fit for presentation on inspection parade. The gate closed behind us, and we were of them—were shut in. No one but those who have had similar experiences can have any conception of the fearful import of those words "shut in." And no pen, however graphic, can give a description that will convey to the uninitiated mind more than the vaguest idea of the horror and misery that centered in the *"Prison Pen at Andersonville."*

My spirit groaned as I stood looking over the crowd of weary, tattered, emaciated forms, that gathered about us eager for news from without. I use the term "weary" as best suited to convey to the mind the haggard, forlorn, absent look imprinted on the countenances of most of those surrounding us. Grasping us by the hands they would ask, "Any news of exchange?"[2]

Exchange! The forlorn hope, the weakening hawser[3] that bound many of them to life, the daystar for whose arising they had so long hoped, almost against hope, and no wonder. The night had been long and dark, the angel of Death had laid a heavy tribute upon them, and his seal was already set upon many more. It was a sickening sight even to me, accustomed as I had been to

---

[1] **stockade**—an enclosure in which prisoners are kept.

[2] exchange—the prisoners are hoping they will be freed in exchange for Confederate prisoners of war freed by the Union.

[3] hawser—a cable or rope used in mooring or towing a ship.

prison horrors. Heretofore, however, my observations had been confined to small numbers—less than a thousand; but here were collected over thirty thousand of the most tattered, dirt-begrimed, squalid-looking men the world ever beheld!

But it was not ours to bring words of comfort, and, as the afternoon was fast passing, we had to busy ourselves in hunting up the squad to which we belonged, as we well knew that upon this depended our getting the little that would be issued to us to eat, and among that multitude it was no small matter to find the sergeant of a squad of ninety men. By diligent inquiry we at last found where it met for roll-call once a day, in the morning. This was near the northeast corner of the stockade. The sergeant, however, was located on the south side.

Having ascertained this much, it became necessary for us to find a place to spend the night,—simply a place to lie down. For you must remember that no shelters were prepared by the Confederate government for our comfort at Andersonville. There were no neat whitewashed houses, such as I had seen at Camp Chase, Ohio, in the prison for Southerners, with its nicely laid-out streets,—none of these. The Confederates having completed the stockade, their only further care was in effect to use the vulgar phrase, "Root, hog, or die," which, simmered down, amounted to this:

"If you can't make yourself a shelter out of nothing, lie out in the rain and dew and hot sun."

Thus I could account for the scant clothing on the men. They would cut off the legs of their trousers and the sleeves of their coats, rip them up, and sew them together to form a shelter from the heat of the sun by day—for it beat with an intenseness against those sand-hills—and the heavy dews at night. The nights being cool, while the earth retained its heat, a very heavy dew was precipitated, sufficient to dampen a person's clothing through. While this might have no **deleterious**[4] effect in one night, a continuation of it through weeks had a marked effect in producing the fearful cases of diarrhea and pneumonia which proved so fatal there.

Many of the boys we noticed had dugouts or subterranean houses, which were treacherous substitutes at best, frequently caving in,—in several instances that came to my knowledge burying the inhabitants alive. As I looked around that evening I noted the many devices made use of in the erection of shelters. I felt that my chances for one were most dubious. Blanket I had none, and no clothing but my shirt, trousers, and blouse, and even if I had had anything to spare, I had no sticks with which to erect a shelter. I felt gloomy enough as I wandered around just as night began to settle around us.

We finally found a place where we could lie, and here Schroeder and I spent our first night in Andersonville. . . .

The earliest light of dawn found me awake, somewhat stiff, but, refreshed by my night's rest, I was ready to start on a tour of investigation. As Schroeder seemed comfortably resting in the embrace of sleep, I did not disturb him, but started out alone. Already the camp showed considerable life. Picking my way among the little shelters scattered irregularly over the ground; now and then stepping over a sleeping form whose bed, like mine, required no particular care; passing an occasional one engaged in preparing his morning meal from the debris of yesterday's rations, and others lost in the earnest effort to make a cup of coffee from burnt crusts, I came to the swamp, which for a time checked further progress until I had seen several of the old inhabitants cross by stepping from clump to clump. It was a terribly filthy place, many going no farther than this to attend to nature's call.

Once across, I came to a squad engaged in performing their morning's **ablutions**.[5] The water in the stream

---

[4] **deleterious**—harmful; injurious.

[5] **ablutions**—a washing or cleansing of the body.

being too filthy for use, they were dipping from a hole that had been dug in the sand near by, into which the water filtered. It was a delightful returning, the air at this early hour being cool and fresh. Asking one of them if he would kindly pour some water onto my hands while I washed, "Certainly, certainly!" he said. After I got through I found I had not taken the wiping into consideration, and began wringing the water from my hands.

"Here," said my new friend, "Use my towel,"— handing me a piece of an old blouse. "How does it come," said he, "that I've never seen you before in here. I thought I had seen all the boys."

I told him that as this was my first appearance on the stage at Andersonville, having only arrived the evening before, it was not remarkable.

"What, just came in?" said he; "where have you been all this time?"

I told him at Danville Hospital.

"Well," he exclaimed, extending his hand, "we'll shake hands then."

My mind was busy at work trying to place him, as it is always embarrassing for one to present himself in that friendly way and then have to introduce himself. Finally I ventured:

"Is it you, Rose?"

"What is left of me, certainly. Why, didn't you know me?"

I never had had any special acquaintance with him, but remembered him as being located near the "Hole in the Wall" at Pemberton Building, Richmond, his feet and mine having been neighbors there when we lay down.

Rose was a representative character. I am sorry I cannot name his regiment. He first attracted my attention in Pemberton by being a close student of his pocket Testament and an observer of its teachings,—

a genuine Christian under adversity, pure gold, tried in the fire. His light had not grown dim through all the ups and downs of prison life.

Leaving Rose, I passed on up the pitch on the east end of south, and sauntered along, thinking the old squad at Pemberton, and directing my steps toward the only two trees that remained in the stockade,—two very large pines near the southeast corner. My course led me close to a fellow who was busy blowing up his fire under his pan (all old prisoners will understand what this means), and my proximity caused him to look up into my face. Then up he jumped and grasped me by the hand with both of his, exclaiming,—"Hello, steward! How are you?"

"Felix, by the life," I exclaimed; "how are you, old boy?"

"Where did you come from?—when did you get in?—where have you been?"—came so rapidly that I had to let him get through before I began,—"as to getting in, why, I arrived last evening."

"In that squad that came in so late?"

"Yes."

"Where did you sleep?"

"Over on the other side."

"Where's your blanket?"

"Have none."

"Didn't sleep out, did you?"

"Have a faint recollection of so doing."

"Why didn't you come over here?"

"Sure enough," I said laughing.

"That's so, that's so," he said, seeing the point. "But here's my tent, I must make room for you under it. My partner was taken out to the hospital yesterday, and you may take his place, although he gave it to another. We must make room for three."

The thanks with which I accepted Felix's hospitality came from a full heart. Here, very unexpectedly to myself, the question of a shelter was settled in a manner that seemed providential. I had not met Felix since I parted with my squad at Pemberton Building for the hospital, nine months before, nine dark, eventful months. How many comrades we could name who had patiently endured the bitterness of Rebel hate, while the wick burned low in its socket, and relief came at last through the gates of Death,—"and yet," said he, "we are still alive." Then, as I made inquiry for this one and that one of our old squad, some had died, several had been exchanged, and several, besides myself, were in Andersonville.

"By the way," he said, "Dick and John, of your regiment, are just down the street in the first tent on the left as you came up the bluff."

I went down immediately, and, stooping down in front of their quarters, whistled. They had not got up yet, but John was awake, and, seeing me, gave Dick a punch or two in the ribs, saying,—

"Dick, Dick, wake up, here's Hyde, the steward!"

Dick needed no second punching, but bounded out in a hurry to meet me. But John, poor fellow, could only hold out his hand. "You'll have to come in to see me," he said, "I can't get up. I can't walk."

He was a German, John Zigler, one of my hospital mess, as was Dick, whose name was Mains, and we had made many a hard day's march together. I could see by his blackened gums and hue that he was fast yielding to scurvy, and, as I learned he was suffering from diarrhea in connection with it, I knew he was correct as he said mournfully, "Well, steward, the jigs are about up with me." Then he showed me his swollen, purple-colored feet, on which the skin shone almost like a mirror, and his limbs drawn up so he could not straighten them. "They will never take me out of here alive," he said. "I know that. I don't know what I would do if I did not have Dick to wait on me and take care of me." No medical man had ever seen him, nor medicine been administered to relieve his sufferings.

Dick and John both said I must come and bunk with them. They had plenty of room, death having made vacancies within a few days. I told them Felix had given me room with him, so I guessed I would remain there; but I had a comrade I would like to shelter with them.

"Bring him right along; he's welcome," was their hospitable invitation.

As the sun was about rising I started to hunt up Schroeder, proud of the success that had attended my ramble, and desirous of introducing him to his new home. I had some difficulty in finding my sleeping-place, as the camp was all astir and the crowd changed the appearance of things. I finally spied him, pacing to and fro on a short beat, his hands clasped behind his back, his favorite attitude when perplexed.

"Mein Gott!" he said, "I am any vay glad to see you once more. Vhen I vaked and found you vas gone I did not know. I thought somebody must have carried you off vhile you slept. Vhere, any vay, have you peen dis early?"

I told him how I had run across Felix, who had kindly given me a place in his tent.

"By jingo," he exclaimed, "dat is goot! I am any vay pleased mit dat."

Then I told him I had faired him a place too, and led the way across the swamp. It seemed as though he had never thought that far ahead, and followed me without saying a word, though I had so studied him that I could tell by the twitching of his facial muscles that he did not dare to express himself just then.

When I got back, Felix was "waiting breakfast for me," as he said I would get hungry before I drew my rations. After breakfast he said:

"Come, let us walk around while it is cool and see the city. There is more to be seen here than you have any idea of, and you will have to see it to realize it. We'll go up to Main Street and walk out toward the south gate, leading off by one of the pine trees along a zigzag way **euphoniously**[6] called Main Street."

While we were slowly walking along, busy in recalling the events of the past nine months, I was suddenly seized by my blouse collar and whirled completely around.

"Can't hear a fellow holler, hey?" was the shout that accompanied a grasp of my hand. I found myself face to face with Williams, a Tennessean, who had been a member of my ward at Danville, and to whom I had given a good blanket when he left for the prison again to be transferred to Andersonville.

"Well, I'm plumb beat this time; why in the world are you in here? I thought you were done exchanged months ago?"

"Haven't been here long? First walk down Main Street," I said.

"Well, it's a mighty hard place. They are killing off a power of the boys; a heap of the Danville boys have done gone since we came here. Have a drink, this is my ranch?"

Dipping down into a barrel, he took up a cup of what he called "beer," but which was nothing more than corn bread and water that had stood until it soured.

"It's not much of a drink," said he; "but it's mighty good for scurvy, and I kind o' like it."

I thought myself it was not much of a drink, but I gulped down a swallow or two out of charity to his good will.

"Come down and see me," continued Williams; "I stay down thar," pointing out his tent.

---

[6] **euphoniously**—pleasingly to the ear.

Felix told him I had come among them entirely destitute, save for what I had on my back.

"Come right down to my tent," reiterated Williams, "I've got an extra cup you can have. I can get along without it. Do you recognize that?" said he, tapping his tent as he stooped to crawl under, "that's the blanket you exchanged with me, and I tell you I've seen the good of it too."

We crawled under the tent and spent some time talking over Danville times and my escape and recapture. Little as these circumstances appear now, they were momentous then, and I love to recall them. Those friendships welded with the hammer of adversity were indissolubly joined, and amid the wreck and ruin of those dark hours they stand forth as bright stars in the depths of ether, each one sending forth its silvery ray to illume the path of memory, and I would not have one of them blotted out until all are swept away together.

"Ah!" said Felix as we passed back to our quarters, "I tell you that's a fine thing,"—pointing to the cup. "I've often felt the need of just such a cup since I've been in here. I tell you it's good and will add to our stock of utensils."

Our water-bucket and soup-pail consisted of boot-tops with wooden bottoms fitted into one end. The signal for roll-call being given, I hastened over to find my squad, and it was no small matter, notwithstanding I thought I had so thoroughly located it in my mind that I would have no difficulty. The sergeant told me my ration would be ready in about two hours, and that I must have something to put it in.

My first ration in Andersonville was a piece of corn bread about as large as the half of an ordinary brick, a small piece of bacon, perhaps three ounces, supposed to be cooked, and half a pint of rice boiled without salt. The bread was simply meal and water mixed and baked without salt. The cooked meat, I noticed, had not been heated hot enough to kill several skippers[7] that flipped out of it.

Felix, like some patriarch of old, was sitting in the door of the tent awaiting my return.

"Well, what did you draw,—something first rate?" he inquired. "A big ration, eh? We'll have to put them together and I will make a 'rolla pot'."

"A what?" I asked.

"A rolla pot," returned he.

"Proceed," I said, "if you know what you are talking about,—I don't."

"That's an Andersonville luxury," replied Felix; "a thing born of circumstances, and I have given it that name for want of a better. You see," he continued, "if you leave that bread until morning it will be sour, so I take out all the soft part and roll it into balls this way,"— suiting the action to the words by rolling the bread in the palms of his hands into balls about an inch in diameter. "These," said he, "I put into some water in the stewpan with some of the meat, and boil the whole together, which makes it all the more palatable and cooks it so that it will keep. Besides," he continued, "you'll find most of the meat we draw is so strong that you can't eat it. A little of the rice, added to the soup, makes that endurable and helps to fill up. Then I have the crust left to make coffee."

While he prepared the "rolla pot" I busied myself in splitting out some pine slats about an inch wide and eight inches long, which I wove together after the fashion of basket splints, and made me a substitute for a plate. This was the only plate I had while I remained in the stockade. For a fork I used a sharpened stick, and for a knife a stick made into a wooden spatula which answered all ordinary purposes, as we had no occasion for carving. I found I had been very fortunate in becoming one of Felix's household, in more ways

---

[7] skippers—insects.

than one. Being one of the "original settlers," he had secured a pine stump, roots and all. This he had stored behind his tent, next to the dead line, where he could watch it, every splinter being valuable. When we got through cooking we gathered up every particle of wood and put out the fire, laying the charred embers carefully away till next time. That you may better get an idea of the value of fuel I will note a little conversation between us to that point.

"What are those fellows doing over there in the swamp?" said I, one day, directing Felix's attention to a dozen or more persons who were wading around in the mire and filth, fuddling around with their arms buried up to their shoulders and feeling carefully as if in search of buried treasures.

"Why," he said, "they are hunting for red-roots to cook with."

"Red-roots!" I echoed,—I suppose in a doubting tone.

"Yes, red-roots. When we first came in here that swamp was covered thick with red-wood bushes as high as your head, or higher, and so thick that a rabbit could not get through them. Now it is as you see,— every inch has been worked over dozens of times, two feet below the surface, in search of bits of roots to cook with. Tough, isn't it?"

Tough! Good Heavens! Think of those fellows thus working over those four or five acres of filthy swamp in search of the smallest fibres of roots, while just outside the stockade walls on the east and south were thousands of cords of the best of pine wood, and hundreds of cords of tree-tops the butts of which had been felled in preparing the pen. These tree-tops had been dragged off the prison ground, and now lay outside, going to waste, although the prisoners would gladly have collected them if they could have had permission to do so, under guard. With teams this valuable fuel could have been brought inside and divided so as to give all an opportunity of working over their ration. The only excuse the authorities vouchsafed for not permitting this was that too many of the boys got away, and that they traded and became too intimate with the guards and might plan an outbreak. Weak **subterfuges!**[8] If they had but said, "It is not the will of the Confederate government that you have that much added to your comfort," they would have struck the nail square on the head, for that is the only reason those poor fellows had to gather roots from the swamp. I made it my business to investigate all that when I was out on parole, and I could attribute the whole thing to nothing but "cussed meanness," well studied and scrupulously applied. There is not a person who was confined there but will testify that the condition of the men might have been bettered a hundredfold without one cent of cost to the Confederate government.

Owing to the bad condition of the water supply the boys had dug a number of wells, some of them forty and fifty feet deep. The sand was of such a character it did not cave in a perpendicular wall. The digging was all done with knives, and the dirt was drawn up in boot-tops. Of course the sand favored the work, but to supply so great a number with good drinking-water was beyond the power of the wells, and there was considerable suffering, with no hopes of anything better as the weather became hotter and the grounds outside became filthier.

---

[8] **subterfuges**—deceptive strategies.

QUESTIONS TO CONSIDER

1. What "crime" have the prisoners at Andersonville committed?

2. What are some of the things that the prisoners do to make their lives at Andersonville more bearable?

3. In what ways could conditions at Andersonville have been improved "without one cent of cost to the Confederate government"?

Leaders

A British Journalist Calls on Jefferson Davis

BY WILLIAM HOWARD RUSSELL

Russell had been a correspondent for the London Times *during the Crimean War (1853–1856) and had shown he could write clearly and insightfully about war in distant places. So, when news of what is going on in America reaches London, the editors of the* Times *send him there. Russell keeps a diary of his trip. It begins shortly after Lincoln's inauguration in 1861. After spending a month in Washington, he sets out for the South and is on board a train when word comes that Fort Sumter has been attacked. By May 9, he has made his way to Montgomery, Alabama, the first capital of the Confederate States of America. Here, in the company of Alabama Senator Wigfall, he calls on the President of the Confederacy.*

May 9th—Today the papers contain a proclamation by the President of the Confederate States of America, declaring a state of war between the Confederacy and the United States, and notifying the issue of letters of marque and reprisal.[1] I went out with Mr. Wigfall in the forenoon to pay my respects to Mr. Jefferson Davis at the State Department. Mr. Seward told me that but for Jefferson Davis the Secession plot could never have been carried out. No other man of the party had the brain, or the courage and dexterity, to bring it to a successful issue. All the persons in the Southern States spoke of him with admiration, though their forms of speech and thought generally forbid them to be respectful to any one.

. . . We walked straight upstairs to the first floor, which was surrounded by doors opening from a quadrangular platform. On one of these was written simply, "The President." Mr. Wigfall went in, and after a moment returned and said, "The President will be glad to see you; walk in, sir." When I entered, the President was engaged with four gentlemen, who were making some offer of aid to him. He was thanking them "in the name of the Government." Shaking hands with each, he saw them to the door, bowed them and Mr. Wigfall out, and turning to me said, "Mr. Russell, I am glad to welcome you here, though I fear your appearance is a symptom that our affairs are not quite prosperous," or words to that effect. . . .

I had an opportunity of observing the President very closely: he did not impress me as favorably as I had expected, though he is certainly a very different looking man from Mr. Lincoln. He is like a gentleman—has a slight, light figure, little exceeding middle height, and holds himself erect and straight. He was dressed in a rustic suit of slate-colored stuff, with a black silk handkerchief round his neck; his manner is plain, and rather reserved and drastic; his head is well-formed,

---

[1] letters of marque and reprisal—licenses to outfit ships for capturing enemy merchant vessels.

with a fine full forehead, square and high, covered with innumerable fine lines and wrinkles, features regular, though the cheek-bones are too high, and the jaws too hollow to be handsome; the lips are thin, flexible, and curved, the chin square, well-defined; the nose very regular, with wide nostrils; and the eyes deep set, large and full—one seems nearly blind, and is partly covered with a film, owing to excruciating attacks of **neuralgia**[2] and tic. Wonderful to relate, he does not chew,[3] and is neat and clean-looking, with hair trimmed and boots brushed. The expression of his face is anxious, he has a very haggard, care-worn, and pain-drawn look, though no trace of anything but the utmost confidence and greatest decision could be detected in his conversation. He asked me some questions respecting the route I had taken in the States.

I mentioned that I had seen great military preparations through the South, and was astonished at the **alacrity**[4] with which the people sprang to arms. "Yes, sir," he remarked, . . . "In Europe" (Mr. Seward also indulges in that pronunciation) "they laugh at us because of our fondness for military titles and displays. All your travelers in this country have commented on the number of generals, and colonels, and majors all over the States. But the fact is, we are a military people, and these signs of the fact were ignored. We are not less military because we have had no great standing armies. But perhaps we are the only people in the world where gentlemen go to a military academy, who do not intend to follow the profession of arms."

. . . Mr. Davis made no allusion to the authorities at Washington, but he asked me if I thought it was supposed in England there would be war between the two States? I answered that I was under the impression the

---

[2] **neuralgia**—sharp, severe pain extending along a nerve or group of nerves.

[3] chew—use chewing tobacco.

[4] **alacrity**—speed.

public thought there would be no actual hostilities. "And yet you see we are driven to take up arms for the defense of our rights and liberties."

As I saw an immense mass of papers on his table, I rose and made my bow, and Mr. Davis, seeing me to the door, gave me his hand and said, "As long as you may stay among us you shall receive every facility it is in our power to afford to you, and I shall always be glad to see you." Colonel Wigfall was outside, and took me to the room of the Secretary of War, Mr. Walker, whom we found closeted with General Beauregard[5] and two other officers in a room full of maps and plans. He is the kind of man generally represented in our types of a "Yankee"—tall, lean, straight-haired, angular, with fiery, impulsive eyes and manner—a ruminator[6] of tobacco and a profuse spitter—a lawyer, I believe, certainly not a soldier; ardent, devoted to the cause, and confident to the last degree of its speedy success.

The news that two more States had joined the Confederacy, making ten in all, was enough to put them in good humor. "Is it not too bad these Yankees will not let us go our own way, and keep their cursed Union to themselves? If they force us to it, we may be obliged to drive them beyond the Susquehanna." Beauregard was in excellent spirits, busy measuring off miles of country with his compass, as if he were dividing empires.

From this room I proceeded to the office of Mr. Benjamin, the Attorney-General of the Confederate States, the most brilliant perhaps of the whole of the famous Southern orators. He is a short, stout man, with a full face, olive-colored, and most decidedly Jewish features, with the brightest large black eyes, one of

---

[5] General Beauregard—Pierre Gustave Toutant Beauregard (1818–1893) was a leading Confederate general. He commanded Confederate troops at Charleston, where he initiated the bombardment of Fort Sumter. He also played a major role in the first Battle of Bull Run.

[6] ruminator—one who chews (chewing tobacco).

which is somewhat diverse from the other, and a brisk, lively, agreeable manner, combined with much vivacity of speech and quickness of utterance. He is one of the first lawyers or advocates in the United States, and had a large practice at Washington, where his annual receipts from his profession were not less than £8,000 to £10,000 a year. But his love of the card-table rendered him a prey to older and cooler hands, who waited till the sponge was full at the end of the session, and then squeezed it to the last drop.

Mr. Benjamin is the most open, frank, and cordial of the Confederates whom I have yet met. In a few seconds he was telling me all about the course of Government with respect to **privateers**[7] and letters of marque and reprisal, in order probably to ascertain what were our views in England on the subject. I observed it was likely the North would not respect their flag, and would treat their privateers as pirates. "We have an easy remedy for that. For any man under our flag whom the authorities of the United States dare to execute, we shall hang two of their people."

"Suppose, Mr. Attorney-General, England, or any of the great powers which decreed the abolition of privateering, refuses to recognize your flag?"

"We intend to claim, and do claim, the exercise of all the rights and privileges of an independent sovereign State, and any attempt to refuse us the full measure of those rights would be an act of hostility to our country."

"But if England, for example, declared your privateers were pirates?"

"As the United States never admitted the principle laid down at the Congress of Paris, neither have the Confederate States. If England thinks fit to declare

---

[7] **privateers**—commanders or crew of a ship authorized by a government during wartime to attack and capture enemy vessels.

privateers under our flag pirates, it would be nothing more or less than a declaration of war against us, and we must meet it as best we can."

In fact, Mr. Benjamin did not appear afraid of anything; but his confidence respecting Great Britain was based a good deal, no doubt, on his firm faith in her cotton interest and manufactures. . . .

Being invited to attend a levee or reception held by Mrs. Davis, the President's wife, I returned to the hotel to prepare for the occasion. On my way I passed a company of volunteers, 120 artillerymen, and three fieldpieces, on their way to the station for Virginia, followed by a crowd of "citizens" and Negroes of both sexes, cheering vociferously. The band was playing that excellent quick-step "Dixie." The men were stout, fine fellows, dressed in coarse grey tunics with yellow facings, and French caps. They were armed with smooth-bore muskets, and their knapsacks were unfit for marching, being waterproof bags slung from the shoulders. The guns had no caissons,[8] and the shoeing of the troops was certainly deficient in soling.

The modest villa in which the President lives is painted white—another "White House"—and stands in a small garden. The door was open. A colored servant took in our names, and Mr. Browne presented me to Mrs. Davis, whom I could just make out in the *demi-jour*[9] of a moderately-sized parlor, surrounded by a few ladies and gentlemen, the former in bonnets, the latter in morning dress *à la midi*.[10] There was no affectation of state or ceremony in the reception. Mrs. Davis, whom some of her friends call "Queen Varina," is a

---

[8] caissons—horse-drawn vehicles, usually two-wheeled, used to carry artillery ammunition; or large boxes used to hold ammunition.

[9] *demi-jour*—in French, literally half-day. Here it refers to an alcove or enclosed space.

[10] *á la midi*—appropriate for midday.

comely, sprightly woman, verging on **matronhood,**[11] of good figure and manners, well-dressed, lady-like, and clever, and she seemed a great favorite with those around her, though I did hear one of them say, "It must be very nice to be the President's wife, and be the first lady in the Confederate States." Mrs. Davis . . . was just now inclined to be angry, because the papers contained a report that a reward was offered in the North for the head of the arch rebel Jeff Davis. "They are quite capable, I believe," she said, "of such acts." There were not more than eighteen or twenty persons present, as each party came in and stayed only for a few moments, and, after a time, I made my bow and retired. . . .

At sundown, amid great cheering, the guns in front of the State Department fired ten rounds, to announce that Tennessee and Arkansas had joined the Confederacy.

In the evening I dined with Mr. Benjamin and his brother-in-law, a gentleman of New Orleans, Colonel Wigfall coming in at the end of dinner. The New Orleans people of French descent, or "Creoles," as they call themselves, speak French in preference to English, and Mr. Benjamin's brother-in-law labored considerably in trying to make himself understood in our **vernacular.**[12] The conversation, Franco-English, very pleasant, for Mr. Benjamin is agreeable and lively. He is certain that the English law authorities must advise the Government that the blockade of the Southern ports is illegal so long as the President claims them to be ports of the United States. "At present," he said, "their paper blockade does no harm; the season for shipping cotton is over; but in October next, when the Mississippi is floating cotton by the thousands of bales, and all our wharves are full, it is inevitable that the Yankees must come to trouble with

---

[11] **matronhood**—being a woman of a mature age and established social position.

[12] **vernacular**—everyday language (that is, English).

this attempt to coerce us." Mr. Benjamin walked back to the hotel with me, and we found our room full of tobacco-smoke, **filibusters,**[13] and conversation. . . .

---

[13] **filibusters**—long speeches.

QUESTIONS TO CONSIDER

1. Why does Mr. Benjamin appear to be unworried about interference from Great Britain?

2. Do you imagine that William Howard Russell will write a flattering or unflattering article about the Confederate States of America? Explain your answer.

3. Which of the people that he meets does Russell seem to like the most? Which does he seem to like the least? Explain.

Grant and Unheroic Leadership

BY JOHN KEEGAN

In his book The Mask of Command, *military historian John Keegan compared the leadership styles of several famous generals in world history. Here he describes General Ulysses S. Grant at the beginning of the battle of Shiloh. Unlike many generals, Grant is not glamorous, dashing, handsome, nor commanding-looking. He is often not very well groomed, and to look at him, you would not think you were looking at one of the greatest generals of all times.*

In the early light of a spring morning during the presidency of Abraham Lincoln, a small man on a large horse was galloping through the dense woodland beside the Tennessee river that led inland from its western shore. The brim of a battered slouch hat nearly met the whiskers of his tight, determined, bearded face. A rough soldier's coat covered his shoulders. Only the knot of staff officers riding in his headlong wake marked him out as a commanding general from the throng of Union soldiers, some ranked in formed units, many leaderless and **fugitive**,[1] that filled the clearings and broken ground through which all moved. The air was charged with the sound of heavy gunfire, sharp-shooting, haphazard volleys, ripples of ordered musketry and the boom of artillery firing **salvoes**[2] at pointblank range. Overhead the leaves pattered with the ripple of passing shots.

The small man was Ulysses Simpson Grant,[3] commanding the District of West Tennessee, the date, April 6, 1862, and the noise, the opening exchanges of the battle of Shiloh, which had broken out some two hours earlier. Behind Grant lay the steamer that had just brought him from his headquarters eight miles downstream. Ahead raged an encounter between the Union and Confederate forces in the western theatre of operations of the American Civil War that had caught him by surprise, cast his army into disorder and thrown the outcome of the North's campaign on the Mississippi headquarters into sudden doubt.

For many men on both sides this was their first battle; for some it was the first occasion on which they had handled firearms. Hundreds of the Northerners had already found the experience of close-order, close-range fighting too much for their manhood and were streaming back, in numbers too large for any intervening officer to check, to temporary safety under the high banks of the Tennessee. Others had stood their ground or yielded it with soldierly reluctance, but in many places they kept their place in the line only by cowering

---

[1] **fugitive**—wandering.

[2] **salvoes**—simultaneous discharge of numerous rounds of ammunition: bombs, bullets, cannonballs, etc.

[3] Keegan is in error when he refers to Grant as Ulysses Simpson Grant. His middle name was Hiram, but a mistake during his admission to West Point resulted in his name being recorded as Ulysses Simpson Grant, and he could not get it corrected. So it stuck with him most of his life. He allowed the middle initial S. but said it "stood for nothing."

in the shelter of earthworks stout enough to breast the hail of shot that swept the ranks. At one spot an observer saw thirty or forty Northerners, each clutching the belt of the man in front, tailing back behind a single thick tree "while a distracted company officer, unable to control himself or his men, paced insanely back from end to end."

The cry at many points was for ammunition. The Southern attack had caught the Northerners with what ball and powder they had had in their pouches, sixty rounds at most, and much of that had been shot off or spilled in the first hour of attack. The Northern army, which could draw on the **copious**[4] output of New England industry, was careless with ammunition at the best of times. In crisis, it expended its ready stocks **prodigally**.[5] It had done so now and Grant, as he began his ride around his stricken front, heeded the cries for ammunition first. He knew that the Southerners, always strapped for supplies, could win a firefight only as a result of bad Northern management of their own superior resources.

The necessary orders given, Grant turned his horse to ride along his front and survey its state. He found confusion that threatened collapse. The fighting had begun before dawn, when patrols from his leading divisions, expecting an unopposed advance into Southern-held territory, had bumped into strong forces of Confederates advancing to attack his main body in its encampment. The patrols had exchanged fire with the Confederate vanguard and then fallen back on their main line. That was composed of regiments almost all fresh to battle, led by officers as innocent of bloodshed as their men. One of them, the 53rd Ohio, had lost its colonel after the second volley. Howling "Fall back and

---

[4] **copious**—plentiful; abundant.

[5] **prodigally**—recklessly wasteful.

save yourselves," he beat many of his soldiers in the race to safety. Another, the 71st Ohio, saw its colonel put spurs to horseflesh the moment the enemy appeared. The colonel of a third, the 6th Iowa, was palpably drunk, unable to give orders and had to be put under arrest by his brigadier. Whether he had been drunk all night or got drunk over breakfast was not established. Either state was perfectly credible in the first year of the Civil War.

Even the best of Grant's subordinates were in trouble. Sherman, who would go marching through Georgia two years later, had had a horse shot under him and suffered a wound in his hand. The Confederates were trying to work round the open flank of his division and were pressing him hard. Prentiss, in the center, was already being forced back. The divisions on the left were giving ground along the river bank. At Pittsburg Landing, where Grant had disembarked, runaways were pressing for shelter into an ever tighter mass under the high bank. There would be 5,000 there by mid-afternoon—some said 15,000—perhaps a fifth of Grant's entire army, many weaponless and none with any stomach for more fighting.

Those whom bravery, coercion or lack of opportunity to flee kept in the line—many more would have run but for the presence of cavalry or broken ground to their rear—were undergoing the most horrible of experiences. One regiment, the 55th Illinois, that did try to break back across a narrow ravine were caught in the hollow and shot down in dozens. "I never saw such cruel work in the war," said a Mississippi major. He spoke for a Confederate army which scented victory and was led forward by a general, A.S. Johnston, whose star stood as high as any Southern soldier's. Its infantry whooped and yelled their way through the woodland; even the artillery, pushing their guns to the edge of the firing line, were fighting like skirmishers. One gun team, unlimbering[6] amid the broken ranks of a fleeing Union regiment, poured salvoes of grape into the fugitives as they streamed past, its victims too terror-stricken to halt, though there were enough of them "to pick up gun, carriage, caisson and horses and hurl them into the Tennessee."

Grant's artillery showed no such spirit. One demoralized gun crew flogged its horses bloody in an attempt to free a cannon jammed solid with a tree trunk between wheel and barrel. A whole battery, terrorized by the detonation of the ready-use ammunition in a limber, put their horses to and galloped clean off the battlefield. Where Grant saw such disorders he intervened to check them. But he could not be everywhere at once and his line, throughout the late morning and early afternoon, was pushed steadily backward, pivoting on its river flank and threatening eventually to be driven into the waters.

He had sent urgently for reinforcements, whose arrival would turn the tide. But the nearest were half a day distant and quite unalerted to the danger with which he coped meanwhile. Until they arrived, he could only gallop here and there, dealing with each crisis as he came to it. This was not one of those battlefields on which European generals expected to practice their craft, a swarth of grassland or open plough, like Waterloo or even Gaugamela.[7] It was a tract of territory, indeed, on which no European army would ever have offered or given battle, a tangle of forest and scrub that denied a discerning eye all chance to survey the fighting line in its entirety.

Smoke filled its rides and hollows, thickets distorted and deflected the noise of gunfire that shredded leaf and

---

[6] unlimbering—removing a gun from a transport vehicle.

[7] The author, British military historian Keegan, is comparing the American Civil War to other wars he has studied.

branch, streams and swamp separated unit from unit. There were no landmarks, no inhabitants to point the way, no *Feldherrnhügel* from which commander and staff could catch a prospect of friend and foe locked in combat. It was an entirely American landscape, one of those wildernesses which settlement as yet had scarcely touched, and Grant, like a native trapper, pioneer or man of the woods, had to deal with it in an entirely American way. A European general would have sounded retreat at the first hint of trouble, thinking to regroup on safer ground and fight another day. He, oppressed by the knowledge that the Union could afford to take "no backward step" in its struggle with Southern rebellion, banished all thought of retreat and rode like fury from blind spot to blind spot, keeping his men in place.

Not all, even in the regiments that showed real fight, could stick their ground. Grant's center division had been driven back early in the day but had then rooted itself on a spot that favored defense. Its strength was whittled away in a succession of Confederate attacks. Its dead strewed its front, its wounded straggled away to the makeshift hospitals hastily organized in the army's rear. But its line remained unbroken. Grant visited it several times during the afternoon, bringing reinforcements when he could find them and heartening its commander with words of encouragement. But as the day wore on, its flanks became exposed, the Southerners working round on left and right to separate the division from its neighbors. Eventually it stood almost surrounded, reduced from 5,000 fighting men to little more than 2,000 and, when the enemy ran guns forward to sweep its front at close range, it could resist no longer. Grant had last visited it at 4:30. At 5:30 the white flag was raised and the survivors gave themselves up.

Fortune favored the brave. The Southern commander had been killed in the attack in the center and his subordinates had not taken the trouble to impede

Grant's closing of the gap in his line the **capitulation**[8] had opened. They had not detected, either, that the Union artillery commander had been massing his surviving artillery on the river flank, where they chose to make what they judged would be the final assault. When unleashed, this assault was devastated by salvoes of grape at close range and dispersed in confusion.

The time was a little after 6. Grant then was close to the river himself, where the reinforcements he had urgently summoned nine hours earlier had begun to disembark in strength. Their appearance put new heart into him and the men about him. A fusspot subordinate, riding up with news that a third of the army was dead, wounded or fugitive, asked if he wanted to issue orders for a withdrawal. Grant dismissed him with curt contempt. Dark was falling, cold sheets of rain had begun to sweep the forest, the battlefield was filled with shivering, shelterless soldiers as anxious for a bite of hot food as they were for an end to the ceaseless bursts of firing which had driven them from one nameless spot to another throughout that awful day. But he, like they, could now glimpse hope of a change of fortunes.

Later that night, Sherman, his West Point classmate, found him standing under a dripping tree, coat collar round his ears, cigar clenched between his teeth. He had come, like the ill-advised subordinate earlier, to speak of retreat. "Some wise and sudden instinct" prompted him otherwise. "Well, Grant," he said. "We've had the devil's own day, haven't we."

Grant took a pull on his cigar, the glow illuminating his neat, tight, determined features. "Yes," said Grant. "Yes. Lick 'em tomorrow, though."

So he did. The greatest general of the American Civil War had begun his ascent from obscurity.

---

[8] **capitulation**—the act of surrendering.

QUESTIONS TO CONSIDER

1. In what way was Grant an "unheroic" leader? What are some of the qualities that made Grant a great general?

2. What factors make the battle at Shiloh different from the typical battles fought by European generals?

3. Although his army suffered tremendous losses on the first day at Shiloh, Grant remained optimistic about the outcome of the battle. Why?

The Emancipation Proclamation

BY ABRAHAM LINCOLN

This historic document did not free all the slaves; it took the Thirteenth Amendment to do that. But it did mean that the Union forces had the power to free slaves wherever the Union took control in the South and that they could accept freed slaves into the military. The Proclamation also meant that the United States now claimed their fight was a moral fight.

Whereas, on the twenty-second day of September, in the year of our Lord one thousand eight hundred and sixty-two, a proclamation was issued by the President of the United States, containing, among other things, the following, to wit:[1]

"That on the first day of January, in the year of our Lord one thousand eight hundred and sixty-three, all persons held as slaves within any state or designated part of a state, the people whereof shall then be in

---

[1] to wit—that is to say.

rebellion against the United States, shall be then, thenceforward, and forever, free; and the Executive Government of the United States, including the military and naval authority thereof, will recognize and maintain the freedom of such persons, and will do no act or acts to repress such persons, or any of them, in any efforts they may make for their actual freedom.

"That the Executive will, on the first day of January aforesaid, by proclamation, designate the states and parts of states, if any, in which the people thereof, respectively, shall then be in rebellion against the United States; and the fact that any state, or the people thereof, shall on that day be in good faith represented in the Congress of the United States, by members chosen thereto at elections, wherein a majority of the qualified voters of such states shall have participated, shall, in the absence of strong countervailing testimony, be deemed conclusive evidence that such state, and the people thereof, are not then in rebellion against the United States."

Now, therefore, I, Abraham Lincoln, President of the United States, by virtue of the power in me vested as commander-in-chief of the army and navy of the United States, in time of actual armed rebellion against the authority and government of the United States, and as a fit and necessary war measure for suppressing said rebellion, do, on this first day of January, in the year of our Lord one thousand eight hundred and sixty-three, and in accordance with my purpose so to do, publicly proclaimed for the full period of one hundred days from the day first above mentioned, order and designate as the states and parts of states wherein the people thereof, respectively, are this day in rebellion against the United States, the following, to wit:

Arkansas, Texas, Louisiana (except the parishes of St. Bernard, Plaquemines, Jefferson, St. John, St. Charles, St. James, Ascension, Assumption, Terre Bonne,

Lafourche, St. Mary, St. Martin, and Orleans, including the city of New Orleans), Mississippi, Alabama, Florida, Georgia, South Carolina, North Carolina, and Virginia (except the forty-eight counties designated as West Virginia, and also the counties of Berkeley, Accomac, Northampton, Elizabeth City, York, Princess Ann, and Norfolk, including the cities of Norfolk and Portsmouth), and which excepted parts are for the present left precisely as if this proclamation were not issued.

And by virtue of the power and for the purpose aforesaid, I do order and declare that all persons held as slaves within said designated states and parts of states are, and henceforward shall be, free; and that the Executive Government of the United States, including the military and naval authorities thereof, will recognize and maintain the freedom of said persons.

And I hereby enjoin upon the people so declared to be free to abstain from all violence, unless in necessary self-defense; and I recommend to them that, all cases when allowed, they labor faithfully for reasonable wages.

And I further declare and make known that such persons, of suitable condition, will be received into the armed service of the United States to garrison forts, positions, stations, and other places, and to man vessels of all sorts in said service.

And upon this act, sincerely believed to be an act of justice, warranted by the Constitution upon military necessity, I invoke the considerate judgment of mankind and the gracious favor of Almighty God.

In witness whereof, I have hereunto set my hand and caused the seal of the United States to be affixed.

Done at the city of Washington this first day of January, in the year of our Lord one thousand eight hundred and sixty-three, and of the Independence of the United States of America the eighty-seventh.

QUESTIONS TO CONSIDER

1. By the terms of the Emancipation Proclamation, what happens to the men, women, and children held as slaves in states not engaged in battle against the Union?

2. What does Lincoln ask of the slaves in return for their freedom?

3. Some argue that the Emancipation Proclamation proves that Lincoln was a courageous leader. Others say that it reveals his chief weakness: an unwillingness to take a firm stand on the issue of slavery. Which side do you agree with and why?

Soldiers for the Union Company E, 4th U.S. Colored Infantry, at Fort Lincoln.
▼

Wartime

Family Support An African-American family enters Union lines bringing supplies to their troops.
▼

General Grant's Council of War This scene near Massaponax Church, Virginia, on May 21, 1864, shows General Grant with his military advisors. Grant is in the foreground looking over General Mead's shoulder. They are studying a map. The photograph was taken by Timothy H. O'Sullivan. ▶

Guns of the Confederate water battery at Warrington, FL.
▼

The cannon known as "Dictator." ▶

Conscription Both the Confederacy, in 1862, and the Union, in 1863, passed conscription laws that required certain men to fight in the war. Both laws allowed wealthier people to avoid combat by paying a fee. In the North, riots broke out as frustrated people expressed their resentment. Here police attack the rioters in New York City.

▲

Irish immigrants, who feared job competition from freed slaves, used the anti-draft riots as an excuse to beat African Americans. This illustration is from *Harper's Weekly* for October 15, 1864.

▲
A ward in the Carver General Hospital, Washington, D.C.

Wounded soldiers in the field after the Battle of Chancellorsville,
May 2, 1863. ▶

Prisoners captured in the Shenandoah Valley being guarded in a
Union camp, May 1862. ▶

Andersonville Union prisoners wait for their food rations
at the infamous Andersonville Prison in Georgia, August 17, 1864.
▼

▲
Three Confederate prisoners from the
Battle of Gettysburg, July 1863.

Lincoln Speaks at Gettysburg

BY CARL SANDBURG

Poet, biographer, historian, and novelist, Carl Sandburg was fascinated by Abraham Lincoln. He wrote a six-volume biography entitled Abraham Lincoln: The War Years. *Here, Sandburg relates the events surrounding the day Lincoln gave his historic "Gettysburg Address." The speech Lincoln gave at the dedication of the cemetery at Gettysburg has become a classic. Lincoln didn't think it was a very good speech, but Edward Everett, the main speaker on that occasion, told him "I wish that I could flatter myself that I had come as near to the central idea of the occasion in two hours as you did in two minutes."*

A printed invitation came to Lincoln's hands notifying him that on Thursday, November 19, 1863, exercises would be held for the dedication of a National Soldiers' Cemetery at Gettysburg. In the helpless onrush of the war too many of the fallen had lain as neglected cadavers rotting in the open fields or thrust into so shallow a resting-place that a common farm plow caught in their bones. Now by order of Governor Curtin of Pennsylvania seventeen acres had been purchased on Cemetery Hill, where the Union center stood its colors on the second and third of July, and plots of soil had been allotted each State for its graves.

The sacred and delicate duties of orator of the day had fallen on Edward Everett, perhaps foremost of all distinguished American classical orators. Serene, suave, handsomely **venerable**[1] in his sixty-ninth year, a prominent specimen of Northern upper-class distinction, Everett was a natural choice of the Pennsylvania commissioners, who sought an orator for a solemn national occasion.

Lincoln meanwhile, in reply to the printed circular invitation, sent word to the commissioners that he would be present at the ceremonies. This made it necessary for the commissioners to consider whether the President should be asked to deliver an address when present.

And so on November 2 David Wills of Gettysburg, as the special agent of Governor Curtin and also acting for the several States, by letter informed Lincoln that the several States having soldiers in the Army of the Potomac who were killed, or had since died at hospitals in the vicinity, had procured grounds for a cemetery and proper burial of their dead. "These grounds will be consecrated and set apart to this sacred purpose by appropriate ceremonies on Thursday, the 19th instant. I am authorized by the Governors of the various States to invite you to be present and participate in these ceremonies, which will doubtless be very imposing and solemnly impressive. It is the desire that after the oration, you, as Chief Executive of the nation, formally set apart these grounds to their sacred use by a few appropriate remarks."

---

[1] **venerable**—worthy of respect.

Lincoln's personal touch with Gettysburg, by tele-graph, mail, courier, and by a throng of associations, made it a place of great realities to him. Just after the battle there, a woman had come to his office, the door-man saying she had been "crying and taking on" for several days trying to see the President. Her husband and three sons were in the army. On part of her husband's pay she had lived for a time, till money from him stopped coming. She was hard put to scrape a living and needed one of her boys to help.

The President listened to her, standing at a fire-place, hands behind him, head bowed, motionless. The woman finished her plea for one of her three sons in the army. He spoke. Slowly and almost as if talking to himself alone the words came and only those words:

"I have two,[2] and you have none."

He crossed the room, wrote an order for the military discharge of one of her sons. On a special sheet of paper he wrote full and detailed instructions where to go and what to say in order to get her boy back.

In a few days the doorman told the President that the same woman was again on hand crying and taking on. "Let her in," was the word. She had located her boy, camp, regiment, company. She had found him, yes, wounded at Gettysburg, dying in a hospital, and had followed him to the grave. And, she begged, would the President now give her the next one of her boys?

As before he stood at the fireplace, hands behind him, head bent low, motionless. Slowly and almost as if talking to himself alone the words came and as before only those words:

"I have two, and you have none."

---

[2] Lincoln is thinking of his two sons at home with him.

He crossed the room to his desk and began writing. As though nothing else was to do she followed, stood by his chair as he wrote, put her hand on the President's head, smoothed his thick and disorderly hair with motherly fingers. He signed an order giving her the next of her boys, stood up, put the priceless paper in her hand as he choked out the one word, "There!" and with long quick steps was gone from the room with her sobs and cries of thanks in his ears.

By many strange ways Gettysburg was to Lincoln a fact in crimson mist.

Fifteen thousand, some said 30,000 or 50,000, people were on Cemetery Hill for the exercises on November 19. On the platform sat governors, major generals, foreign Ministers, members of Congress, officials, together with Colonel Ward Hill Lamon, Edward Everett and his daughter, and the President of the United States.

The United States House chaplain offered a prayer while the thousands stood with uncovered heads.

Benjamin B. French, officer in charge of buildings in Washington, introduced the Honorable Edward Everett, orator of the day, who rose, bowed low to Lincoln, saying, "Mr. President." Lincoln responded, "Mr. Everett."

The orator of the day then stood in silence before a crowd that stretched to limits that would test his voice. Beyond and around were the wheat fields, the meadows, the peach orchards, long slopes of land, and five and seven miles farther the contemplative blue ridge of a low mountain range. His eyes could sweep them as he faced the audience. He had taken note of it in his prepared and rehearsed address. "Overlooking these broad fields now **reposing**[3] from the labors of the **waning**[4] year, the mighty Alleghanies

---

[3] **reposing**—resting.
[4] **waning**—approaching an end.

dimly towering before us, the graves of our brethren beneath our feet, it is with hesitation that I raise my poor voice to break the eloquent silence of God and Nature. But the duty to which you have called me must be performed,—grant me, I pray you, your indulgence and your sympathy." He spoke for an hour and fifty-seven minutes, some said a trifle over two hours, repeating almost word for word an address that occupied nearly two newspaper pages, as he had written it and as it had gone in advance sheets to many newspapers.

Everett came to his closing sentence without a faltering voice: "Down to the latest period of recorded time, in the glorious annals of our common country there will be no brighter page than that which relates THE BATTLES OF GETTYSBURG." It was the effort of his life and embodied the perfections of the school of oratory in which he had spent his career. His erect form and sturdy shoulders, his white hair and flung-back head at dramatic points, his voice, his poise, and chiefly some quality of inside goodheartedness, held most of his audience to him, though the people in the front rows had taken their seats three hours before his oration closed.

Having read Everett's address, Lincoln knew when the moment drew near for him to speak. He took out his own manuscript from a coat pocket, put on his steel-bowed glasses, stirred in his chair, looked over the manuscript, and put it back in his pocket. Ward Hill Lamon rose and spoke the words "The President of the United States," who rose, and holding in one hand the two sheets of paper at which he occasionally glanced, delivered the address in his high-pitched and clear-carrying voice.

The Gettysburg Address
by Abraham Lincoln

Fourscore and seven years ago, our fathers brought forth upon this continent a new nation, conceived in liberty and dedicated to the proposition that all men are created equal.

Now we are engaged in a great civil war, testing whether that nation—or any nation, so conceived and so dedicated—can long endure.

We are met on a great battle-field of that war. We are met to dedicate a portion of it as the final resting place of those who have given their lives that that nation might live.

It is altogether fitting and proper that we should do this.

But, in a larger sense, we cannot dedicate, we cannot consecrate, we cannot hallow, this ground. The brave men, living and dead, who struggled here, have consecrated it, far above our power to add or to detract.

The world will very little note nor long remember what we say here; but it can never forget what they did here.

It is for us, the living, rather, to be dedicated, here, to the unfinished work that they have thus far so nobly carried on. It is rather for us to be here dedicated to the great task remaining before us; that from these honored dead we take increased devotion to that cause for which they here gave the last full measure of devotion; that we here highly resolve that these dead shall not have died in vain; that the nation shall, under God, have a new birth of freedom, and that government of the people, by the people, for the people, shall not perish from the earth.

* * *

The applause, according to most of the responsible witnesses, was formal and perfunctory, a tribute to the occasion, to the high office, to the array of important men of the nation on the platform, by persons who had sat as an audience for three hours. Ten sentences had been spoken in five minutes, and some were surprised that it should end before the orator had really begun to get his outdoor voice.

The ride to Washington took until midnight. Lincoln was weary, talked little. He had stood that day, the world's foremost spokesman of popular government, saying that democracy was yet worth fighting for. He had spoken as one in mist who might head on deeper yet into mist. He **incarnated**[5] the assurances and pretenses of popular government, implied that it could and might perish from the earth. What he meant by "a new birth of freedom" for the nation could have a thousand interpretations. The taller riddles of democracy stood up out of the address. It had the dream touch of vast and furious events epitomized for any foreteller to read what was to come. He did not assume that the drafted soldiers, substitutes, and bounty-paid privates had died willingly under Lee's shot and shell, in deliberate consecration of themselves to the Union cause. His cadences sang the ancient song that where there is freedom men have fought and sacrificed for it, and that freedom is worth men's dying for. For the first time since he became President he had on a dramatic occasion declaimed, howsoever it might be read, Jefferson's proposition which had been a slogan of the Revolutionary War— "All men are created equal"—leaving no other inference than that he regarded the Negro slave as a man. His outwardly smooth sentences were inside of them gnarled and tough with the **enigmas**[6] of the American experiment.

---

[5] **incarnated**—personified.

[6] **enigmas**—things that are puzzling, ambiguous, or inexplicable.

Back at Gettysburg the blue haze of the Cumberland Mountains had dimmed till it was a blur in a nocturne. The moon was up and fell with a bland golden benevolence on the new-made graves of soldiers, on the **sepulchers**[7] of old settlers, on the horse carcasses of which the onrush of war had not yet permitted removal.

In many a country cottage over the land, a tall old clock in a quiet corner told time in a tick-tock deliberation. Whether the orchard branches hung with pink-spray blossoms or icicles of sleet, whether the outside news was seed-time or harvest, rain or drought, births or deaths, the swing of the pendulum was right and left and right and left in a tick-tock deliberation.

The face and dial of the clock had known the eyes of a boy who listened to its tick-tock and learned to read its minute and hour hands. And the boy had seen years measured off by the swinging pendulum, and grown to man size, had gone away. And the people in the cottage knew that the clock would stand there and the boy never again come into the room and look at the clock with the query, "What is the time?"

In a row of graves of the Unidentified the boy would sleep long in the dedicated final resting-place at Gettysburg. Why he had gone away and why he would never come back had roots in some mystery of flags and drums, of national fate in which individuals sink as in a deep sea, of men swallowed and vanished in a man-made storm of smoke and steel.

The mystery deepened and moved with ancient music and inviolable consolation because a solemn Man of Authority had stood at the graves of the Unidentified and spoken the words "We cannot

---

[7] **sepulchers**—burial vaults.

consecrate—we cannot **hallow**[8]—this ground. The brave men, living and dead, who struggled here, have consecrated it, far above our poor power to add or detract. . . . From these honored dead we take increased devotion to that cause for which they gave the last full measure of devotion."

To the backward and forward pendulum swing of a tall old clock in a quiet corner they might read those cadenced words while outside the windows the first flurry of snow blew across the orchard and down over the meadow, the beginnings of winter in a gun-metal **gloaming**[9] to be later arched with a star-flung sky.

---

[8] **hallow**—to make or set apart as holy.

[9] **gloaming**—twilight or dusk.

QUESTIONS TO CONSIDER

1. Why do you think Sandburg includes the story of the woman who seeks to have one of her boys discharged from the army?

2. Who is the boy who grew up in the cottage with the tall clock?

3. What are the main differences between Mr. Everett's speech at Gettysburg and President Lincoln's address?

4. In your opinion, what is the most important point Lincoln makes in the Gettysburg Address?

Lee's Final Order

BY NANCY SCOTT ANDERSON
AND DWIGHT ANDERSON

The day following the surrender at Appomattox Court House in Virginia, General Robert E. Lee issued his final order to his troops. Joshua Chamberlain, the Union officer assigned to conduct the formal ceremony called "stacking of arms," remembers the day and the deep feelings of sorrow and pride he felt.

It was raining that afternoon as Grant saddled up and rode out of Appomattox Court House. It was still raining the following day when Lee issued his final order to his troops:

> After four years of arduous service, marked by unsurpassed courage and fortitude, the Army of Northern Virginia has been compelled to yield to overwhelming numbers and resources.

> I need not tell the brave survivors of so many hard fought battles, who have remained steadfast

to the last, that I have consented to the result from no distrust of them.

But feeling that valor and devotion could accomplish nothing that would compensate for the loss that must have attended the continuance of the contest, I determined to avoid the useless sacrifice of those whose past services have endeared them to their countrymen.

By the terms of the agreement officers and men can return to their homes and remain until exchanged. You will take with you the satisfaction that proceeds from the consciousness of duty faithfully performed, and I earnestly pray that a Merciful God will extend to you His blessing and protection.

With an increasing admiration of your constancy and devotion to your country, and a grateful remembrance of your kind and generous considerations for myself, I bid you all an affectionate farewell.

Lee could have gone, but he stayed. He needed to finish the war up and wait until his army was a thing of the past. The men knew he waited in his tent during the last review.

Joshua Chamberlain conducted the formal stacking of arms and he never forgot it. "It was now the morning of the 12th of April," he wrote. "I had been ordered to have my lines formed for the ceremony at sunrise. It was a chill gray morning, depressing to the senses. But our hearts made warmth. Great memories uprose; great thoughts went forward. We formed along the principal street, from the bluff bank of the stream to near the Court House on the left,—to face the last line of battle, and receive the last remnant of the arms and colors of the great army which ours had been created to confront for all that death can do for life. We were remnants also: Massachusetts, Maine, Michigan, Maryland, Pennsylvania, New York; veterans, and replaced veterans; cut to pieces, cut down, consolidated, divisions into brigades, regiments into one . . . men of near blood born, made nearer by blood shed. Those facing us—now, thank God! the same. . . .

"Our earnest eyes scan the busy groups on the opposite slopes, breaking camp for the last time, taking down their little shelter-tents and folding them carefully as precious things, then slowly forming ranks as for unwelcome duty. And now they move. The dusky swarms forge forward into gray columns of march. On they come, with the old winging route step and swaying battle flags . . . crowded so thick, by thinning out of men, that the whole column seemed crowned with red. . . .

"Before us in proud humiliation stood the embodiment of manhood: men whom neither toils and sufferings, nor the fact of death nor disaster, nor hopelessness could bend from their resolve; standing before us now, thin, worn, and famished, but erect, and with eyes looking level into ours, waking memories that bound us together as no other bond. . . ."

Without official sanction, and all unplanned, Chamberlain suddenly gave the order for the Union soldiers to "order arms"[1] in that deepest mark of military respect. "Gordon at the head of the column, riding with heavy spirit and downcast face, catches the sound of shifting arms, looks up, and, taking the meaning, wheels superbly, making with himself and his horse one uplifted figure, with profound salutation as he drops the point of his sword to the boot toe." Gordon ordered

---

[1] order arms—a position in which the rifle is held at the right side, with its butt on the ground.

his men to respond in kind—"honor answering honor. On our part not a sound . . . but an awed stillness rather, and breath-holding, as if it were the passing of the dead!

"As each successive division masks our own, it halts, the men face inward towards us across the road, twelve feet away; then carefully 'dress' their line. . . . They fix bayonets, stack arms; then, hesitatingly, remove cartridge-boxes and lay them down. Lastly—reluctantly, with agony of expression—they tenderly fold their flags, battle-worn and torn, blood-stained, heart-holding colors, and lay them down. . . .

"What visions thronged as we looked into each other's eyes! Here pass the men of Antietam, the Bloody Lane, the Sunken Road, the Cornfield . . . The men who swept away the Eleventh Corps at Chancellorsville; who left six thousand of their companions around the bases of Culp's and Cemetery Hills at Gettysburg; these survivors of the terrible Wilderness, the Bloody Angle at Spotsylvania, the slaughter pen of Cold Harbor!

"Here comes Cobb's Georgia Legion. . . . Here too comes Gordon's Georgians and Hoke's North Carolinians, who stood before the terrific mine explosion at Petersburg, and advancing retook the smoking crater[2] and the dismal heaps of dead—ours more than theirs—huddled in the ghastly chasm.

"Now makes its last front A.P. Hill's old Corps, Heth now at the head, since Hill had gone too far forward ever to return; the men who poured destruction into our division at Sherpardstown Ford, Antietam, in 1862 . . . the men who opened the desperate first day's fight at Gettysburg. . . .

"Now the sad great pageant—Longstreet and his men: What shall we give them for greeting that has not already been spoken in volleys of thunder and written

---

[2] retook the smoking crater—see "The Crater" by J. Power on page 123.

in lines of fire on all the riverbanks of Virginia? . . . Now comes the sinewy remnant of fierce Hood's Division. . . .

"Ah, is this Pickett's Division?—this little group left of those who on the lurid last day of Gettysburg breasted level crossfire and thunderbolts of storm to be strewn back drifting wrecks, where after that awful, futile, pitiful charge we buried them in graves a furlong[3] wide, with names unknown!

"Met again in the terrible cyclone-sweep over the breastworks of Five Forks; met now, so thin, so pale, purged of mortal,—as if knowing pain or joy no more.

"How could we help falling on our knees, all of us together, and praying God to pity and forgive us all!"

---

[3] furlong—unit for measuring distance, equal to ⅛ mile (201 meters).

QUESTIONS TO CONSIDER

1. What is Lee's final order?

2. Why does Chamberlain tell his men to "order arms"?

3. In what ways are the two groups of men—Union and Confederate—now similar?

Aftermath

Lincoln's Assassination

BY RICHARD BAK

On the evening of April 14, 1865, a well-known actor named John Wilkes Booth stole into a private box at Ford's Theater, pointed a derringer pistol at the back of the head of Abraham Lincoln, and squeezed the trigger. By morning, the sixteenth president of the United States was dead. In the following excerpt from The Day Lincoln Was Shot, *biographer Richard Bak vividly re-creates this momentous event.*

It was sometime around 10:15, with the third act in progress. Booth had been in and out of the theater several times while the play was in progress, leaving to fortify himself with a stiff drink of whiskey before returning. In the alley, Edman Spangler was supposed to be holding the reins of his mare. Now, Booth's frenzied preparations earlier in the day were about to pay off. That afternoon, while the theater was empty, he had bored a finger-sized peephole in the inner door to the box. This gave him a perfect view of the back of

Lincoln's rocking chair. He'd also gouged a **mortise**[1] in the plaster wall opposite the door leading into the corridor. By bracing a wooden bar between the door and the wall, he was able to prevent anyone from rushing through the jammed door. From under his coat he pulled a .44 caliber derringer pistol and a nine-inch knife.

Mary Lincoln would give two different accounts of her husband's last words. At first, she remembered that she had been leaning close to him, her hand on his knobby knee, and said playfully, "What will Miss Harris think of my hanging on to you so?" To which Lincoln replied: "She won't think anything about it."

Her other version had the president, perhaps waking from some private daydream, improbably saying, "How I should like to visit Jerusalem sometime!"

In the play, comic lead Harry Hawk played Asa Trenchard, an American backwoodsman trying to pass himself off as a millionaire. Hawk was alone on the stage when he responded to the gold-digging mother who had just discovered he was as poor as a church mouse. "Don't know the manners of good society, eh?" he said. "Well, I guess I know enough to turn you inside out, old gal—you sockdologizing old mantrap!"

Hawk was looking in Mrs. Lincoln's direction as he delivered the lines. He would always remember that she was smiling at the very moment a shot rang out in the president's box.

Long seconds of quiet bewilderment were followed by outright **pandemonium.**[2] Edwin Emerson was standing in the wings, waiting for his cue to go on, when he heard the cra-a-ck! of a pistol. He described the delayed reaction and ensuing chaos:

I was not surprised, nor was anyone else behind the scenes. Such sounds are too common during

---

[1] **mortise**—a hole, groove, or slot.
[2] **pandemonium**—a wild uproar.

the shifting of the various sets to surprise an actor. For a good many seconds after that sound nothing happened behind the footlights. Then, as I stood there in the dimness, a man rushed by me, making for the stage door. I did not recognize Booth at the time, nor did anyone else, I think, unless perhaps someone out on the stage, when he stood a moment and shouted with theatrical gesture, *Sic Semper Tyrannis!* (So perish all tyrants!)" Even after he flashed by, there was quiet for a few moments among the actors and the stage hands. No one knew what had happened.

Then the fearful cry, springing from nowhere it seemed, ran like wildfire behind the scenes:

"The President's shot!"

Everyone began to swirl hither and thither in hysterical aimlessness. Still the curtain had not been rung down—for no one seemed to have retained a **scintilla**[3] of self-possession—and the actors on the stage were left standing there as though paralyzed.

Then someone dropped the curtain and pandemonium commenced. The police came rushing in to add to the chaos, and for what seemed an hour, the confusion was indescribable. One incident stands out plainly in my memory from the confusion of men and sound that turned the stage into chaos. As I was running aimlessly to and fro behind the scenes—as everyone else was—a young lady, coming out from a dressing room, asked the cause of all the uproar.

---

[3] **scintilla**—spark; trace.

"President Lincoln has just been shot!" I replied.

"Oh!" she exclaimed and, closing her eyes, was sinking limp to the floor in a faint when I caught her and carried her into her dressing room. She was Miss Jennie Gourlay, one of the then well-known family of actors, and that night playing the part of Mary Trenchard.

"Booth, being an actor, was familiar with the stage," actress Katherine Evans, who was inside the dressing room with Gourlay, told the *New York Tribune* years later:

He ran between Hawk and Billy Ferguson, struck at [William] Withers, our orchestra leader, with his knife, and made his way out through the stage door into the alley where "Peanut Johnnie" the boy who sold peanuts in the gallery was holding his horse.

I looked and saw President Lincoln unconscious, his head dropping on his breast, his eyes closed, but with a smile still on his face. Mrs. Lincoln had risen from her seat beside him and was stroking his cheeks. . . .

In an instant the theater was in an uproar. It was crowded to the top-most gallery, and every one had risen in his seat. Men were shouting and climbing out into the aisles. Miss Keene was making her way up to where the president lay wounded, and several doctors from the audience were trying to force a passage through the crowd. Dr. Charles Taft was lifted up into the box from the stage, while many persons, some of them physicians, were crowding into the narrow aisle which led into the box and were pounding on the door, demanding admission.

The **report**[4] of the derringer "seemed to proceed from behind the President's box," remembered Dr. Taft, who was enjoying the play from his front row seat:

> While it startled everyone in the audience, it was evidently accepted by all as an introductory effect preceding some new situation in the play, several of which had been introduced in the earlier part of the performance. A moment afterward a hatless and white-faced man leaped from the front of the president's box down twelve feet to the stage. As he jumped, one of the spurs on his riding boots caught in the folds of the flag dropped over the front, and caused him to fall partly on his hands and knees as he struck the stage. Springing quickly to his feet with the suppleness of an athlete, he faced the audience for a moment as he brandished in his right hand an Iona knife, and shouted *"Sic Semper Tyrannis!"* Then, with a rapid stage stride, he crossed the stage, and disappeared from view. A piercing shriek from the president's box, a repeated call for "Water! water!" and "A surgeon!" in quick succession, conveyed the truth to the almost paralyzed audience. A most terrible scene of excitement followed. With loud shouts of "Kill him!" "Lynch him!" part of the audience stampeded towards the entrance and some to the stage.
>
> I leaped from the top of the orchestra railing in front of me upon the stage, and, announcing myself as an army surgeon, was immediately lifted up to the president's box by several gentlemen who had collected beneath. . . .

---

[4] **report**—the noise made when a pistol is fired.

When I entered the box, the president was lying upon the floor surrounded by his wailing wife and several gentlemen who had entered from the private stairway and dress circle. Assistant Surgeon Charles A. Leale . . . had caused the coat and waistcoat to be cut off in searching for the wound. Dr. A.F.A. King of Washington was also present, and assisted in the examination. The carriage had been ordered to remove the president to the White House, but the surgeons countermanded the order, and he was removed to a bed in the house opposite the theater. . . .

All in all, the assassination had gone smoothly. Booth had quietly opened the inner door of the box, crept up behind the president's chair, and fired his derringer at point-blank range at the left side of Lincoln's head. The ball crashed through his skull behind the left ear, then tunneled its way diagonally across the brain before stopping behind his right eye. Lincoln's head slumped forward, his whiskered chin resting on his chest. He never regained consciousness.

Before anybody in the box could really react, Booth had pushed his way between the president and Mrs. Lincoln. Major Rathbone, confused, jumped off the sofa and began grappling with the dark-clothed assailant. Booth slashed at Rathbone with his knife, a blow the officer parried with his left arm. The blade inflicted a terrible wound, slicing the officer's arm all the way to the bone. Booth then jumped from the box onto the stage, a leap he had made many times as an actor, stopping just long enough to make a declaration. There is no agreement as to Booth's exact words—a cruel irony for a seasoned **thespian**[5] who had undoubtedly chosen his parting lines with great care and with an eye to history.

---

[5] **thespian**—actor.

After his utterance, the nineteenth-century Brutus[6] in knee-high riding boots and spurs darted into the night, leaving behind a gas-lit cauldron of confusion.

At about the same time that Booth was leveling his derringer at the back of Lincoln's head, Lewis Powell[7] was singlehandedly turning the secretary of state's house on Lafayette Park, just across from the White House, into a war zone. Having talked his way past a servant and through the front door with the story that he was delivering medicine for Seward, he was met with skepticism by the secretary's son, Frederick. Agreeing to leave, Powell suddenly pulled out a revolver and fired. When it failed to go off, he crashed it down on Frederick's head, shattering his skull and the pistol.

Pulling out a large Bowie knife, Powell rushed up the stairs to Seward's bedroom. Fanny Seward, the secretary's fragile twenty-one-year-old daughter, was knocked unconscious with a single powerful blow. An army nurse, Sergeant George Robinson, was thrown aside before Powell jumped on the secretary's bed. In the dimly lit room Powell thrust again and again into Seward's face, looking to slash his jugular. Luckily for Seward, he was wearing a brace that deflected several of the blows. Robinson and another of Seward's sons, Major Augustus Seward, pulled Powell off. In the ensuing struggle, Augustus was stabbed seven times and Robinson four. The assailant ran out the front door shouting, "I'm mad! I'm mad!" On his way out he plunged his knife into the chest of Emerick Hansell, a messenger who had innocently stumbled onto the carnage.

Powell had been a one-man wrecking crew, leaving five badly slashed and beaten victims in his wake. All would survive, though the secretary would carry

---

[6] Brutus—assassin of a great leader. The author is referring to the senator who stabbed Julius Caesar.

[7] Lewis Powell—one of Booth's fellow conspirators.

horrible scars on his face for the rest of his life and his daughter would never fully recover from the trauma, passing away the following year. . . .

Dr. Charles A. Leale, only two months out of medical school, was the first doctor to reach Lincoln. "Oh, doctor," cried Mary Lincoln, "do what you can for my dear husband! Is he dead? Can he recover?" Leale spotted the clot behind the left ear. He removed it, then dug his finger into the opening. Blood flowed and the breathing became more regular.

Leale was quickly joined by more physicians. It was clear that there was nothing much that could be done for the president. He was paralyzed and his pulse was weak. "His wound is mortal," said Leale. "It is impossible for him to recover."

The decision was made to take the president to the nearest bed. Across the street, a young boarder directed that he be brought into the house of William Petersen, a German tailor who was his landlord. With blood and brain matter seeping out his wound and half of his clothes cut off, the once vital figure of Abraham Lincoln was carried into a small bedroom at the end of the first-floor hallway. It turned out that his six-foot, four-inch frame was too long for the bed. Unable to break the footboard off, Dr. Leale directed that his body be placed diagonally across the mattress. That is how Lincoln spent the last nine hours of his life, his large, bare feet sticking out by the wall, his swelling, discolored, bleeding head propped up on two large pillows.

Charles Sumner, the abolitionist senator from Massachusetts, hurried to the Petersen House with the president's oldest son, Robert. Sumner took the president's hand in his.

"It's no use," one of the doctors said. "He can't hear you. He is dead."

"No, he isn't dead," insisted Sumner desperately. "Look at his face, he's breathing."

"It will never be anything more than this," the doctor said.

Robert Lincoln wept and Sumner put his arm around him, waiting, like all the rest, for the end to finally come. Outside it was raining. Upwards of ninety different people made their way into the cramped bedroom at one time or another. These included sixteen doctors who were frantic to try anything—mustard plasters, hot water bottles, blankets—to keep him warm and his great heart beating, and a hysterical Mary Lincoln, whose shrieking finally got her removed for good at three in the morning. At times the only sounds were the raindrops tapping the windowpane and the ominous ticking of the dock The passing seconds boomed like artillery inside the still room. There was nothing to do but to wait and pray. Dr. Leale kept the president's hand in his throughout, "so that in the darkness he would know he had a friend," he explained.

Finally, at 7:22 A.M., Lincoln slipped away.

QUESTIONS TO CONSIDER

1. What factors aided Booth and caused the assassination to go smoothly?

2. What does Booth's motive for killing the president appear to have been?

3. What might account for the variations in the reports of eyewitnesses to Lincoln's assassination?

The Thirteenth, Fourteenth, and Fifteenth Amendments

The most immediate and greatest legacy of the Civil War was the end of slavery. The United States Congress passed the Thirteenth Amendment, ending slavery, in January, 1865, four months before the war's end. However, it took until December for the states to **ratify**[1] *it. The Fourteenth Amendment, passed in June, 1866, and ratified just over two years later, established that Americans are citizens of both the nation and the states, and that states cannot deny them the privileges of citizenship. The Fifteenth Amendment granted all men the right to vote.*

AMENDMENT 13. SLAVERY ABOLISHED (1865) Passed by Congress January 31, 1865. Ratified December 6, 1865.

---

[1] **ratify**—approve.

Section 1

Neither slavery nor involuntary servitude, except as a punishment for crime whereof the party shall have been duly convicted, shall exist within the United States, or any place subject to their jurisdiction.

Section 2

Congress shall have power to enforce this article by appropriate legislation.

AMENDMENT 14. CIVIL RIGHTS (1868) Passed by Congress June 13, 1866. Ratified July 9, 1868.

Section 1

All persons born or naturalized in the United States, and subject to the jurisdiction thereof, are citizens of the United States and of the state wherein they reside. No state shall make or enforce any law which shall abridge the privileges or immunities of citizens of the United States; nor shall any state deprive any person of life, liberty, or property, without due process of law; nor deny to any person within its jurisdiction the equal protection of the laws.

Section 2

Representatives shall be apportioned among the several states according to their respective numbers, counting the whole number of persons in each state. But when the right to vote at any election for the choice of electors for President and Vice-President of the United States, Representatives in Congress, the executive and judicial officers of a state, or the members of the legislature thereof, is denied to any of the male inhabitants of such state, and citizens of the United States, or in any way abridged, except for participation in rebellion, or other crime, the basis of representation therein shall be reduced in the proportion which the number of such male citizens shall bear to the whole number of citizens in such state.

Section 3

No person shall be a Senator or Representative in Congress, or elector of President and Vice-President, or hold any office, civil or military, under the United States, or under any state, who, having previously taken an oath, as a member of Congress, or as an officer of the United States, or as a member of any state legislature, or as an executive or judicial officer of any state, to support the Constitution of the United States, shall have engaged in insurrection or rebellion against the same, or given aid or comfort to the enemies thereof. But Congress may, by a vote of two thirds of each house, remove such disability.

Section 4

The validity of the public debt of the United States, authorized by law, including debts incurred for payment of pensions and bounties for services in suppressing insurrection or rebellion, shall not be questioned. But neither the United States nor any state shall assume or pay any debt or obligation incurred in aid of insurrection or rebellion against the United States, or any claim for the loss or emancipation of any slave; but all such debts, obligations and claims shall be held illegal and void.

Section 5

The Congress shall have power to enforce, by appropriate legislation, the provisions of this article.

AMENDMENT 15. RIGHT TO VOTE (1870)
Passed by Congress February 26, 1869. Ratified
February 3, 1870.

Section 1

The right of citizens of the United States to vote shall
not be denied or abridged by the United States or by
any state on account of race, color, or previous condition
of servitude.

Section 2

The Congress shall have power to enforce this article
by appropriate legislation.

QUESTIONS TO CONSIDER

1. After the passage of the Fourteenth Amendment, could
   General Robert E. Lee have been elected President of the
   United States? Explain.

2. Which rights are to be given priority—the rights granted by
   the states or the rights granted to U.S. citizens?

3. What is the purpose of the Fifteenth Amendment?

The Legacy of Defeat

BY GARY W. GALLAGHER

Nearly 250,000 lives lost, cities destroyed, farmlands laid to waste, and a social system in upheaval—these were the results of the war for the South. It left a legacy of bitterness that would take many generations to lessen. Historian Gallagher uses excerpts from letters and diaries to illustrate how the former Confederates felt in war's aftermath.

Testimony from the aftermath of the war reveals unequivocally that most Confederates believed they had been beaten rather than undermined by internal weaknesses. The first sentence of Lee's famous farewell address to his soldiers conveyed this attitude: "After four years of arduous service, marked by unsurpassed courage and fortitude, the Army of Northern Virginia has been compelled to yield to overwhelming numbers and resources." Catherine Edmondston and Sarah Hine typified those who seconded Lee's assessment that the North had overpowered Confederate defenders in the field. North Carolinian Edmondston, who repeatedly had vowed to resist to the bitter end, remarked in her diary that "the Vulgar Yankee nation exults over our misfortunes, places its foot upon our necks, & extols its own prowess in conquering us. They command all the R Roads & other routes of travel & they have the ability to force their detested oath down the throat of every man amongst us."

Georgian Sarah Hine hated the idea of **relinquishing**[1] hope for an independent Confederacy but had no doubt about what had compelled Confederate surrender. "One thing I shall glory in to the latest hour of my life," she wrote, is that "we never yielded in the struggle until we were bound hand & foot & the heel of the **despot**[2] was on our throats." What was the condition of those who yielded to the Federals? "Bankrupt in men, in money, & in provisions," explained Hine, "the wail of the bereaved & the cry of hunger rising all over the land, Our cities burned with fire and our pleasant things laid waste, the best & bravest of our sons in captivity, and the entire resources of our country exhausted—what else could we do but give up."

Graphic evidence supporting Hine's stark catalog greeted anyone traveling through the South after the Confederate surrender. Thousands of graves bespoke the grim toll on a generation of young men. Many of the dead had been interred hastily near where they had fallen, their remains often subject to the ravages of rooting hogs or the elements. Visiting the battlefield at the Wilderness shortly after the war, northern writer John T. Trowbridge described "three or four Rebel graves with old headboards" near a fence corner. "The words indicated that those buried were North Carolinians," observed Trowbridge: "The graves were

---

[1] **relinquishing**—giving up.

[2] **despot**—tyrant; one who exercises power abusively.

shallow, and the settling of the earth over the bodies had left the feet of one of the poor fellows sticking out." Uncertainty about the location of dead relatives heightened the pain of loss in countless southern households, and **ubiquitous**[3] empty sleeves and trouser legs afforded additional reminders of sacrifice in a brutal war.

Major southern cities bore deep scars from the conflict. Photographer George N. Barnard, who followed the route of Sherman's army across Georgia and through the Carolinas, recorded ruined private homes, burned railroad yards, and piles of rubble that once had been public buildings in Atlanta, Columbia, and Charleston. In Richmond, where Confederates had set fire to public facilities as they retreated, photographers trained their cameras on scenes in the vicinity of the state capitol (which had housed the Confederate Congress during most of the war), near the Tredegar Iron Works, and among huge mills along the James River. Their haunting images captured the widespread devastation described by war clerk John B. Jones after a walk through the ruined section of Richmond on April 4, 1865. "Some seven hundred houses, from Main Street to the canal, comprising the most valuable stores, and the best business establishments," stated Jones, "were consumed. All the bridges across the James were destroyed, the work being done effectually." Hundreds of miles of trenches, once occupied by Union and Confederate soldiers seeking shelter from minié balls and artillery projectiles, formed ugly rings around such cities as Petersburg, Richmond, Chattanooga, Atlanta, and Vicksburg, and long sections of field works similarly marred the rural southern landscape.

In addition to the serpentine lines of field works, physical damage comparable to anything in the cities

---

[3] **ubiquitous**—widespread; existing everywhere.

extended across vast stretches of the agricultural South. Wherever armies had camped for any length of time, thousands of hungry campfires had devoured many acres of forests, substituting moonscapes for previously lush vegetation. Long before William Tecumseh Sherman and Philip H. Sheridan struck at logistical production in central Georgia and the Shenandoah Valley during their famous 1864 campaigns (operations often cited by historians to mark the beginning of a harsher phase of war), much of the Confederacy's farming heartland already had experienced catastrophic damage from armies bent on destruction or merely seeking food and fodder for thousands of soldiers and animals.

A half dozen witnesses from Virginia, Tennessee, and Louisiana suggest the degree of civilian dislocation. British observer A. J. L. Fremantle noted in June 1863 that the region along the eastern slope of the Blue Ridge Mountains near Sperryville was "completely cleaned out." The presence of two armies for more than a year had left many acres "almost uncultivated, and no animals are grazing where there used to be hundreds. All fences have been destroyed, and numberless farms burnt, the chimneys alone left standing." Fremantle concluded, "It is difficult to depict and impossible to exaggerate the sufferings which this part of Virginia has undergone." In the fall of 1864, a visitor to Fredericksburg similarly remarked that he saw "not a fence nor an inhabited house" in the surrounding region: "All is still as death for miles and miles under the sweet autumnal sun."

Middle Tennessee presented a comparably bleak picture that mocked its **antebellum**[4] reputation as an agricultural showplace. The region had been overrun by Federal armies in 1862 and subject to wide-scale foraging for most of the war. "This is a dreary, desolate, barren and deserted looking country," observed a Union officer well

---

[4] **antebellum**—pre-war. In the U.S., this word is used to mean "before the Civil War."

before the midpoint of the conflict. "The houses and stores are either closed or smashed to pieces. Everything is going to utter destruction." A northern cavalryman writing in April 1863 anticipated the language Fremantle would use to describe Sperryville two months later: "It is really sad to see this beautiful country here so ruined. There are no fences left at all. There is no corn and hay for the cattle and horses, but there are no horses left anyhow and the planters have no food for themselves." A Confederate passing through the area a few weeks later saw "not a stalk of corn or a blade of wheat growing" and thought "the country wears the most desolate appearance that I have ever seen anywhere."

The valley of the Red River in Louisiana presented an equally dreary picture in mid-1864. Writing to a friend in Texas, Lt. Col. George W. Guess of the 31st Texas Cavalry proclaimed that "not only every **vestige**[5] of food in the whole country has been destroyed, but nearly every town & every house has been burned." Guess reported that women and children had lost everything "& they are in the woods without food, shelter or clothing. There are many that have been in easy circumstances who are actually living on blackberries." None of this came secondhand, affirmed Guest: "These things I know to be true, for I see them with my own eyes. And what a sight!" . . .

Abundant testimony of this type could be marshaled to support the point that by the spring of 1865 the Confederacy had absorbed as much punishment as its people could tolerate. Amid increasing deprivation and against mounting odds during the last seven or eight months of fighting, most Confederates had fixed their eyes on Lee and his army to sustain diminishing hopes for independence. The end of the war found them exhausted, unable to muster a satisfactory answer to Sarah Hines's rhetorical "What else could we do but give up."

---

[5] **vestige**—trace; remaining bit.

. . . Many Confederates expressed continued devotion to their southern nation. Private James A. Scott of the 3rd Virginia Cavalry confessed that he had "much to regret—but it may all be summed up in a word—that I did not do more for my oppressed and unhappy country." Taking comfort from the fact that he had been "able to do even a little" to support the South's fight for independence, Scott insisted that "we were engaged in a just and holy war." He refused to believe so many thousands of Confederates had perished in vain and hoped white southerners would accept their current state of poverty as a challenge to rebuild their troubled land. "We have failed in our efforts to establish a separate nationality," wrote Scott, but "it's hard to think that our glorious old Confederate banner—which we have borne high aloft unconquered so long—must now be furled—but I doubt not—in his own good time God will give us a new & more beautiful one which shall float proudly and wide over all of our foes. Let us put our trust in Him."

. . . Elizabeth Pendleton Hardin, a Kentuckian who had lived in various sections of the Confederacy, expressed a "hope I may never again love anything as I loved the cause that is lost." Leaving Eatonton, Georgia, to return to Kentucky in early June 1865, Hardin and her family shouted "Hurrah for Jeff Davis and the Southern Confederacy" as they waved good-bye to their Georgian friends. "We had been there two years and a half, watching with unfaltering hope our struggle for independence and life," wrote Hardin in her diary, "and now that our hopes had all come to naught, we returned to our homes with sad hearts, feeling we had left the brightest part of our lives behind us. . . ."

Few former Confederates believed the war had proved secession illegal. Armed might alone, rather than constitutional authority, lay behind the North's ability to label former Confederates as traitors. Two witnesses elaborated common themes. John Richard Dennett, who traveled the immediate postwar South as a correspondent for the *Nation,* talked with a man in Richmond who proclaimed that the "people of the South feel that they have been most unjustly, most tyrannically oppressed by the North. All our rights have been trampled upon." Although Confederates had been "subjugated, conquered, and in their collective capacity they must submit to whatever may be inflicted upon them," this man averred that they "had a most perfect right to secede, and we have been slaughtered by the thousands for attempting to exercise it." He added darkly that "the people of the South are not going to stand that." A Unionist judge from Alexandria, Virginia, pointed to similar sentiment among ex-Confederates. "They boast of their treason," he told the Joint Committee on Reconstruction in January 1866, "and ten or eleven out of the twelve on any jury . . . would say that Lee was almost equal to Washington, and was the noblest man in the State, and they regard every man who has committed treason with more favor than any man in the State who has remained loyal to the government." A member of the Committee asked if the judge referred to people across the entire state of Virginia. "Yes, sir," came the reply.

White southerners who retained Confederate loyalties typically harbored deep resentments against Federal soldiers and northerners in general. Although compelled to acknowledge Union success in suppressing their struggle for independence, Confederates defiantly refused to forgive enemies who had inflicted such pain on their society. Elizabeth Hardin and Anne S. Frobel used their diaries to vent hatred for Yankees shared by untold others. "The Psalmist and I are alike in one respect at least," remarked Hardin in a passage rich in biblical allusions. "We both have seen the wicked flourish like a green bay tree and the vilest men exalted."

Hardin wished the French would make trouble for the United States in Mexico: "I would like to cry, 'Vive la France!' I am afraid I would be tempted to cry 'Vive Beelzebub'[6] if he were fighting the Yankees."

Frobel's animosity toward Yankees was such that she believed they arranged accidents to kill Confederate prisoners of war attempting to return south. "I cannot understand how it is that so many Confederate prisoners being sent home are lost," she wrote in frustration and anger. "In every paper we see now there is some terrible account of disaster to Confederates[.] [A]t one place a boat was snagged and two, or three, hundred drowned. Then a train ran off the track, and a great number killed[.] The last account was of a boat load, between Ft Lookout and Savanna being scalded to death by the steams being turned on them (accidentally of course)[.]" More immediately, Union soldiers stationed near Frobel's farm in Fairfax County, Virginia, during the summer of 1865 pulled down fences, drank her well dry, commandeered her stables for their mounts, and generally disrupted her life. "There is no annoyance conceivable that these dreadful people do not inflict on us," she complained. After Union soldiers swarmed around her well and left the water "entirely unfit for use" during a July 4th celebration, Frobel lashed out against the "selfish-miserable wretches" who had acted, she stressed, in typical Yankee fashion.

Northern soldiers frequently commented about the insolence and animosity they perceived among former Confederates. One such observer was Union sergeant Mathew Woodruff, who betrayed reciprocal dislike for white southerners in relating an incident in Mobile, Alabama. When a black woman reprimanded three young girls for waving a rebel flag, the children's mother "appeared with a saucy rebuke & insults to all Yanks,

---

[6] Beelzebub—the devil.

saying 'they' (the South) was not whiped & if they got a chance would rise again." Woodruff believed these "to be the prevailing sentiments throughout the South." He added, "There is not 9 out of 10 of these so called 'Whiped' traitors that I would trust until I saw the rope applied to their Necks, then I would only have Faith in the quality of the rope."

Sergeant Woodruff would have said that the song "O, I'm a Good Old Rebel"—the 1866 sheet music for which was sarcastically dedicated to "the Hon. Thad. Stevens"[7]—accurately reflected widespread feelings among ex-Confederates. Its bitter lyrics combined pride in the Confederacy, recognition that further armed resistance was impossible, and determination to keep alive hatred for the northern foe:

> Three hundred thousand Yankees is stiff in Southern dust.
> We got three hundred thousand before they conquered us.
> They died of Southern fever and Southern steel and shot,
> I wish they was three million instead of what we got.
>
> I can't take up my musket and fight them now no more,
> But I ain't gonna love them, now that is certain sure.
> And I don't want no pardon for what I was and am
> I won't be reconstructed, and I don't care a damn.

---

[7] "the Hon. Thad. Stevens"—a Radical Republican representative from Pennsylvania. He was pro-abolition, pro-war, and pro-rights for former slaves.

QUESTIONS TO CONSIDER

1. What factors made it clear that the Confederacy could no longer continue to fight the war?

2. At war's end, how did most white Southerners feel about the Confederate cause and leaders such as Jefferson Davis and Robert E. Lee?

3. What opinion did the Southerners have of Federal soldiers and Northerners in general?

What War Wrought

The Civil War left the South in ruins. The cities, the countryside, farms, fortunes, and families were destroyed. It took generations to overcome the bitterness that divided the South from the North. Here are the ruins of the mills at Richmond, Virginia in April, 1865.

Ford's Theater This tall building in the middle of the photograph is the playhouse in Washington, D.C., where the assassin John Wilkes Booth took the President's life.

John Wilkes Booth A popular actor, Booth was an ardent Confederate—he had been a volunteer in the Richmond militia that hanged the abolitionist John Brown. After shooting the President, he is said to have called out the Latin phrase, *"Sic semper tyrannis!"* which means "Thus always to tyrants!" It is the Revolutionary War slogan that became Virginia's state motto. Then he jumped to the stage and broke his leg. Though he managed to escape, Federal troops caught up with him eleven days later. He died— whether by his own hand or by that of the troops, no one knows. ▶

▲
This was the last photograph taken of Abraham Lincoln.

◀ **Charleston, S.C.** Ruins seen from the Circular Church in 1865.

Columbia, S.C. View from the capitol building, 1865.
▼

▲
Several generations of one family all born on J.J. Smith's Plantation, Beaufort, S.C. 1862.

◄ **End of Slavery** As the Federal troops won victories, they liberated slaves. But life for the newly freed was not an easy one. The Civil War was only the beginning of a struggle for civil rights that took more than a century to make real gains. This scene is on the James Hopkinson Plantation at Edisto Island, South Carolina.

Poetry and Songs of the Civil War

Great events, including wars, have always inspired poets and songwriters. Poet Walt Whitman helped care for wounded Union soldiers in Washington, D.C., during the Civil War. Here, his "Beat! Beat! Drums!" describes the chaos sounded by the drums of war. Poet Henry Timrod writes of his native city during the Union blockade in the early part of the war in "Charleston." Abolitionist newspaper editor Julia Ward Howe wrote "Battle Hymn of the Republic" to the tune of a Confederate camp song by South Carolinian William Steffe called "John Brown's Body Lies a Mould'ring in the Grave." And New York songwriter and music publisher George Root wrote the stirring "Battle Cry of Freedom" or "We'll Rally Round the Flag, Boys."

Beat! Beat! Drums!

BY WALT WHITMAN

Beat! beat! drums!—blow! bugles! blow!
Through the windows—through doors—burst like a
    ruthless force,
Into the solemn church, and scatter the congregation,
Into the school where the scholar is studying;
Leave not the bridegroom quiet—no happiness must he
    have now with his bride,
Nor the peaceful farmer any peace, plowing his field or
    gathering his grain,
So fierce you whir and pound you drums—so shrill you
    bugles blow.

Beat! beat! drums!—blow! bugles! blow!
Over the traffic of cities—over the rumble of wheels in
    the streets;
Are beds prepared for sleepers at night in the houses? no
    sleepers must sleep in those beds,
No bargainers' bargains by day—no brokers or
    speculators—would they continue?
Would the talkers be talking? would the singer attempt
    to sing?
Would the lawyer rise in the court to state his case
    before the judge?
Then rattle quicker, heavier drums—you bugles
    wilder blow.

Beat! beat! drums!—blow! bugles! blow!
Make no **parley**[1]—stop for no **expostulation**,[2]
Mind not the timid—mind not the weeper or prayer,
Mind not the old man beseeching the young man,

---

[1] **parley**—negotiations between enemies over terms of truce or
other matters.

[2] **expostulation**—earnest protest.

Let not the child's voice be heard, nor the mother's
   entreaties,
Make even the trestles to shake the dead where they
   lie awaiting the hearses,
So strong you thump O terrible drums—so loud you
   bugles blow.

Charleston

BY HENRY TIMROD

Calm as that second summer which precedes
   The first fall of the snow,
In the broad sunlight of heroic deeds
   The City bides the foe.

As yet, behind their **ramparts**[3] stern and proud,
   Her bolted thunders sleep—
Dark Sumter like a **battlemented**[4] cloud
   Looms o'er the solemn deep.

No **Calpe**[5] frowns from lofty cliff or scar
   To guard the holy strand;
But **Moultrie**[6] holds in leash her dogs of war
   Above the level sand.

---

[3] **ramparts**—defensive walls.

[4] **battlement**—the characteristic indentations on the top of a defensive wall.

[5] **Calpe**—ancient name of the Rock of Gibraltar.

[6] **Moultrie**—Fort Moultrie, located at the entrance to the harbor of Charleston, S.C., was the Confederate headquarters for the bombardment of Fort Sumter in April, 1861.

And down the dunes a thousand guns lie couched
    Unseen beside the flood—
Like tigers in some Orient jungle crouched,
    That wait and watch for blood.

Meanwhile, through streets still echoing with trade,
    Walk grave and thoughtful men
Whose hands may one day wield the patriot's blade
    As lightly as the pen.

And maidens with such eyes as would grow dim
    Over a bleeding hound
Seem each one to have caught the strength of him
    Whose sword she sadly bound.

Thus girt without and garrisoned at home,
    Day patient following day,
Old Charleston looks from roof and spire and dome
    Across her tranquil bay.

Ships, through a hundred foes, from Saxon lands
    And spicy Indian ports
Bring Saxon steel and iron to her hands
    And Summer to her courts.

But still, along yon dim Atlantic line
    The only hostile smoke
Creeps like a harmless mist above the brine
    From some frail, floating oak.

Shall the Spring dawn, and she still clad in smiles
    And with an unscathed brow,
Rest in the strong arms of her palm-crowned isles
    As fair and free as now?

We know not: in the temple of the Fates
  God has inscribed her doom;
And, all untroubled in her faith, she waits
  The triumph or the tomb.

Battle Hymn of the Republic

BY JULIA WARD HOWE

Mine eyes have seen the glory of the coming of the Lord:
He is trampling out the vintage where the grapes of
  wrath are stored;
He hath loosed the fateful lightning of his terrible
  swift sword:
        His truth is marching on.

I have seen Him in the watch fires of a hundred circling
  camps;
They have builded Him an altar in the evening dews
  and damps;
I can read His righteous sentence by the dim and flaring
  lamps.
        His day is marching on.

I have read a fiery gospel writ in **burnished**[7] rows of
  steel:

---

[7] **burnished**—polished.

"As ye deal with my **contemners,**[8] so with you my grace
shall deal;
Let the Hero, born of woman, crush the serpent with his
heel,
Since God is marching on."

He has sounded forth the trumpet that shall never call
retreat;
He is sifting out the hearts of men before his judgment
seat:
Oh! be swift, my soul, to answer Him! be jubilant, my
feet!
Our God is marching on.

In the beauty of the lilies Christ was born across the sea,
With a glory in His bosom that transfigures you and me:
As He died to make men holy, let us die to make men
free,
While God is marching on.

[Chorus]
Glory, Glory, hallelujah!
Glory, glory, hallelujah!
Glory, glory, hallelujah!
His truth is marching on.

---

[8] **contemners**—critics; detractors.

Battle Cry of Freedom (*or* We'll Rally Round the Flag, Boys)

BY GEORGE ROOT

Yes we'll rally round the flag, boys, we'll rally once again,
    Shouting the battle cry of freedom,
We will rally from the hill-side, we'll gather from the plain,
    Shouting the battle cry of freedom.

    The Union forever, hurrah, boys, hurrah!
    Down with the traitor, up with the star;
    While we rally round the flag, boys, rally once again,
    Shouting the battle cry of freedom.

We are springing to the call for Three Hundred
  Thousand more,
    Shouting the battle cry of freedom,
And we'll fill the vacant ranks of our brothers gone before,
    Shouting the battle cry of freedom.

    The Union forever, hurrah, boys, hurrah!
    Down with the traitor, up with the star;
    While we rally round the flag, boys, rally once again,
    Shouting the battle cry of freedom.

We will welcome to our numbers the loyal, true, and brave,
    Shouting the battle cry of freedom,
And altho' he may be poor he shall never be a slave,
    Shouting the battle cry of freedom.

The Union forever, hurrah, boys, hurrah!
Down with the traitor, up with the star;
While we rally round the flag, boys, rally once again,
Shouting the battle cry of freedom.

So we're springing to the call from the East and from the
West,
Shouting the battle cry of freedom,
And we'll hurl the rebel crew from the land we love the
best,
Shouting the battle cry of freedom.

The Union forever, hurrah, boys, hurrah!
Down with the traitor, up with the star;
While we rally round the flag, boys, rally once again,
Shouting the battle cry of freedom.

QUESTIONS TO CONSIDER

1. Which of these poems and songs do you think of as
   optimistic? Which seem pessimistic? Explain.

2. Why do you think Julia Ward Howe's "Battle Hymn of
   the Republic" continues to appeal to people more than
   125 years after it was first written?

3. Contrast the tone of Whitman's "Beat! Beat! Drums!"
   with the tone of Root's "Battle Cry of Freedom." Which
   one creates a more vivid picture of the war? Which one
   did you find more moving? Explain.

Grant and Lee: A Study in Contrasts

BY BRUCE CATTON

Bruce Catton is one of America's best-known historians of the Civil War. Catton's essay compares and contrasts the two great Civil War generals. It is often used as a model of great writing, for it joins the character of the man with the character of the region of the country each comes from. Grant, the victor, represents the future, and Lee, the past. It would be interesting to consider how Catton might have written this if the outcome of the war had been different.

When Ulysses S. Grant and Robert E. Lee met in the parlor of a modest house at Appomattox Court House, Virginia, on April 9, 1865, to work out the terms for the surrender of Lee's Army of Northern Virginia, a great chapter in American life came to a close, and a great new chapter began.

These men were bringing the Civil War to its virtual finish. To be sure, other armies had yet to surrender and for a few days the fugitive Confederate government would struggle desperately and vainly, trying to find some way to go on living now that its chief support was gone. But in effect it was all over when Grant and Lee signed the papers. And the little room where they wrote out the terms was the scene of one of the poignant, dramatic contrasts in American history.

They were two strong men, these oddly different generals, and they represented the strengths of two conflicting currents that, through them, had come into final collision.

Back of Robert E. Lee was the notion that the old aristocratic concept might somehow survive and be dominant in American life.

Lee was tidewater Virginia, and in his background were family, culture, and tradition . . . the age of chivalry transplanted to a New World which was making its own legends and its own myths. He embodied a way of life that had come down through the age of knighthood and the English country squire. America was a land that was beginning all over again, dedicated to nothing much more complicated than the rather hazy belief that all men had equal rights, and should have an equal chance in the world. In such a land Lee stood for the feeling that it was somehow of advantage to human society to have a pronounced inequality in the social structure. There should be a leisure class, backed by ownership of land; in turn, society itself should be keyed to the land as the chief source of wealth and influence. It would bring forth (according to this ideal) a class of men with a strong sense of obligation to the community; men who lived not to gain advantage for themselves, but to meet the solemn obligations which had been laid on them by the very fact that they were privileged. From them the country would get its leadership; to them it could look for the higher values—of thought, of conduct, of personal deportment—to give it strength and virtue.

Lee embodied the noblest elements of this aristocratic ideal. Through him, the landed nobility justified itself. For four years, the Southern states had fought a desperate war to uphold the ideals for which Lee stood. In the end, it almost seemed as if the Confederacy fought for Lee; as if he himself was the Confederacy . . . the best thing that the way of life for which the Confederacy stood could ever have to offer. He had passed into legend before Appomattox. Thousands of tired, underfed, poorly clothed Confederate soldiers, long-since past the simple enthusiasm of the early days of the struggle, somehow considered Lee the symbol of everything for which they had been willing to die. But they could not quite put this feeling into words. If the Lost Cause, sanctified by so much heroism and so many deaths, had a living justification, its justification was General Lee.

Grant, the son of a tanner on the Western frontier, was everything Lee was not. He had come up the hard way, and embodied nothing in particular except the eternal toughness and **sinewy**[1] fiber of the men who grew up beyond the mountains. He was one of a body of men who owed reverence and **obeisance**[2] to no one, who were self-reliant to a fault, who cared hardly anything for the past but who had a sharp eye for the future.

These frontier men were the precise opposites of the tidewater aristocrats. Back of them, in the great surge that had taken people over the Alleghenies and into the opening Western country, there was a deep, implicit dissatisfaction with a past that had settled into grooves.

[1] **sinewy**—lean and muscular.

[2] **obeisance**—an attitude of deference or homage.

They stood for democracy, not from any reasoned conclusion about the proper ordering of human society, but simply because they had grown up in the middle of democracy and knew how it worked. Their society might have privileges, but they would be privileges each man had won for himself. Forms and patterns meant nothing. No man was born to anything, except perhaps to a chance to show how far he could rise. Life was competition.

Yet along with this feeling had come a deep sense of belonging to a national community. The Westerner who developed a farm, opened a shop, or set up in business as a trader could hope to prosper only as his own community prospered—and his community ran from the Atlantic to the Pacific and from Canada down to Mexico. If the land was settled, with towns and highways and accessible markets, he could better himself. He saw his fate in terms of the nation's own destiny. As its horizons expanded, so did his. He had, in other words, an acute dollars-and-cents stake in the continued growth and development of his country.

And that, perhaps, is where the contrast between Grant and Lee becomes most striking. The Virginia aristocrat, inevitably, saw himself in relation to his own region. He lived in a static society which could endure almost anything except change. Instinctively, his first loyalty would go to the locality in which that society existed. He would fight to the limit of endurance to defend it, because in defending it he was defending everything that gave his own life its deepest meaning.

The Westerner, on the other hand, would fight with an equal tenacity for the broader concept of society. He fought so because everything he lived by was tied to growth, expansion, and a constantly widening horizon. What he lived by would survive or fall with the nation itself. He could not possibly stand by unmoved in the face of an attempt to destroy the Union. He would combat it with everything he had, because he could only see it as an effort to cut the ground out from under his feet.

So Grant and Lee were in complete contrast, representing two **diametrically**[3] opposed elements in American life. Grant was the modern man emerging; beyond him, ready to come on the stage, was the great age of steel and machinery, of crowded cities and a restless, burgeoning vitality. Lee might have ridden down from the old age of chivalry, lance in hand, silken banner fluttering over his head. Each man was the perfect champion of his cause, drawing both his strengths and his weaknesses from the people he led.

Yet it was not all contrast, after all. Different as they were—in background, in personality, in underlying aspiration—these two great soldiers had much in common. Under everything else, they were marvelous fighters. Furthermore, their fighting qualities were really very much alike.

Each man had, to begin with, the great virtue of utter tenacity and fidelity. Grant fought his way down the Mississippi Valley in spite of acute personal discouragement and profound military handicaps. Lee hung on in the trenches at Petersburg after hope itself had died. In each man there was an **indomitable**[4] quality . . . the born fighter's refusal to give up as long as he can still remain on his feet and lift his two fists.

Daring and resourcefulness they had, too; the ability to think faster and move faster than the enemy. These were the qualities which gave Lee the dazzling campaigns of Second Manassas and Chancellorsville and won Vicksburg for Grant.

---

[3] **diametrically**—directly, completely.
[4] **indomitable**—incapable of being subdued; unconquerable.

Lastly, and perhaps greatest of all, there was the ability, at the end, to turn quickly from war to peace once the fighting was over. Out of the way these two men behaved at Appomattox came the possibility of a peace of reconciliation. It was a possibility not wholly realized, in the years to come, but which did, in the end, help the two sections to become one nation again . . . after a war whose bitterness might have seemed to make such a reunion wholly impossible. No part of either man's life became him more than the part he played in their brief meeting in the McLean house at Appomattox. Their behavior there put all succeeding generations of Americans in their debt. Two great Americans, Grant and Lee—very different, yet under everything very much alike. Their encounter at Appomattox was one of the great moments of American history.

QUESTIONS TO CONSIDER

1. According to Catton, what was Lee's first loyalty?

2. What was Grant's first loyalty?

3. What did Grant and Lee have in common?

4. Why was Grant and Lee's encounter at Appomattox one of the great moments of American history?

1818—Slave and non-slave states are balanced at 10 each.

1820—The Missouri Compromise is adopted.

1838—The Second Annual Meeting of the Anti-Slavery Convention of American Women is mobbed.

1845—Texas statehood permits slavery.

1849—California forbids slavery.

1850—The Compromise of 1850 including the Fugitive Slave Act is enacted.

1852—*Uncle Tom's Cabin* is published.

1854—Kansas–Nebraska Act permits slavery north of 36°30'.

1855—Slavery supporters and abolitionists organize rival governments in Kansas.

1856—Rioting earns the state the name "Bleeding Kansas."

1857—The *Dredd Scott* decision makes the Missouri Compromise unconstitutional.

1858—The Lincoln-Douglas Debates are held in Illinois.

1859—John Brown attacks the Federal arsenal at Harpers Ferry, Virginia.

1860—Abraham Lincoln wins the presidential election. South Carolina secedes.

1861—**February:** The Confederate States of America is formed. A peace convention called by Virginia fails to avert the crisis. Jefferson Davis is elected president of the Confederacy. **April:** Confederates fire on Fort Sumter. **July:** Confederates win the Battle of Bull Run.

1862—**April:** The Battle of Shiloh demonstrates the need for trenches. Admiral Farragut wins at New Orleans. **March 23–June 9:** Stonewall Jackson's tactics in the Shenandoah Valley defeat the larger Union forces. **June 26–July 2:** Lee defeats McClellan in the Seven Days' Battles. **August 29–30:** Lee wins the Second Battle of Bull Run. **September 17:** The bloodiest battle of the war is fought at Antietam. **November 7:** Lincoln fires McClellan. **December:** Lincoln weathers a cabinet crisis.

1863—**January 1:** Lincoln issues the Emancipation Proclamation. **March:** The first conscription act in the United States is passed. **May:** The South wins at Chancellorsville, but Jackson is killed. Grant lays siege to Vicksburg. **July:** Lee loses the Battle of Gettysburg. Vicksburg falls to Grant. Draft riots rage in New York City. **August:** Farragut closes the port at Mobile Bay, Alabama. **October:** Grant, given command of armies in the west, begins a drive to split the Confederacy. **November:** Lincoln gives the Gettysburg Address.

1864—**May:** Grant, given command in the east, begins a slow drive in Virginia with the Battle of the Wilderness. Sherman begins his march through Georgia. **June:** Grant lays siege to Petersburg, south of Richmond. **September and October:** Sheridan lays waste to the Shenandoah Valley. **November:** Sherman burns Atlanta. Lincoln wins a second term as President. **December:** Sherman takes Savannah.

1865—**January through March:** Sherman begins a destructive march through South and North Carolina. **March:** The Union forces approach Richmond. **April:** President Davis and his government abandon the capitol. Lee surrenders on April 9. Lincoln is assassinated on April 14. **May:** Sherman defeats the Confederates in North Carolina. Confederate forces in New Orleans surrender, ending Southern resistance. **December:** Twenty-seven states ratify the Thirteenth Amendment, abolishing slavery in the United States.

27 "Lucretia Mott Faces a Mob" by Margaret Hope Beacon from *Quaker History*, 82, Fall, 1993. Reprinted by permission of Friends Historical Association.

47 "Florida Passes the Ordinance of Secession" from *Through Some Eventful Years* by Susan Bradford. Macon: J. W. Burke Company, 1926.

66 "Letters from a Sharpshooter" by William B. Greene from *Letters From A Sharpshooter 1861-1865* transcribed by William H. Hastings, 1993. Reprinted by permission of the University Press of Virginia and William H. Hastings.

81 "Diary of Wartime" by Cornelia Peake McDonald from *A Diary with Reminiscences of the War and Refugee Life in the Shenandoah Valley, 1860-1865* by Hunter McDonald. (Nashville: Cullom & Ghertner, 1934.)

118 "The Colored Troops" from *Voices From The Civil War* by Milton Meltzer. Copyright © 1989 by Milton Meltzer. Used by permission of HarperCollins Publishers.

123 "The Crater" from *Lee's Miserables: Life in the Army of Northern Virginia From The Wilderness to Appomattox* by J. Tracy Power. Copyright © 1998 by the University of North Carolina Press. Used by permission of the publisher.

154 "Grant and Unheroic Leadership" from *The Mask of Command* by John Keegan. Copyright © 1987 by John Keegan. Used by permission of Viking Penguin, a division of Penguin Putnam Inc.

176 "Lincoln Speaks at Gettysburg" from *Abraham Lincoln: The Prairie Years and The War Years* by Carl Sandburg. Copyright 1926 by Harcourt Brace & Company and renewed 1954 by Carl Sandburg. Reprinted by permission of the publisher.

185 "Lee's Final Order" from *The Generals: Ulysses S. Grant and Robert E. Lee* by Nancy Scott Anderson and Dwight Anderson. Copyright © 1987 by Nancy Scott Anderson and Dwight Anderson. Reprinted by permission of Alfred A. Knopf, Inc.

192 "Lincoln's Assassination" from *The Day Lincoln Was Shot* by Richard Bak. Copyright © 1998 by Richard Bak. Reprinted by permission of Taylor Publishing Company.

205 "The Legacy of Defeat" reprinted by permission of the publisher from *The Confederate War* by Gary W. Gallagher, Cambridge, Mass.: Harvard University Press, Copyright © 1997 by the President and Fellows of Harvard College.

230 "Grant and Lee: A Study in Contrasts" by Bruce Catton. Copyright U. S. Capitol Historical Society. All rights reserved. Reprinted by permission.

Photo Research Diane Hamilton

Photos Courtesy of the Library of Congress and the National Archives.

Every effort has been made to secure complete rights and permissions for each selection presented herein. Updated acknowledgements, if needed, will appear in subsequent printings.

Index